Thank You for Listening

Listening

Gain Influence & Improve Relationships
Better Listening Skills in 8 Steps

Marc Wong

Cover speech bubble image Copyright Petr Vaclavek, 2012. Used under license from Shutterstock.com

DEDICATION

This book is dedicated to my parents.

CONTENTS

ACKNOWLEDGMENTS

The events in my life and more importantly the people who have helped me along the way have all made this book possible. I wish to thank Dr. Patrick and Monique Chan, Raymond and Suzy Koo, Felicia and Lynette Son-hing, Anthony and Dawn Son-hing, Quintin and Lana Son-hing, Gary and Wee Lee Wong, Dr. Gordon McLennan, Velma Hunter, Dr. Art McDonald, Donna Noftle, Dr. Carolyn Smart, Dr. William T. Thompson, Jeff and Lily Lee, Matthew Chang, Tom and Garbo Chow, Lowin Yeung, Andrew Leung, Christine Greybe, Richard Liscio, Jim Krantz, Michael Amoroso, Jonathan Klein, Sanjay Maljure, Premanand Gupta, Gregg Davis, Henry and Shirley Fok, Cecilia Kwong, Christopher Simmons, and of course my editors M.P. Feitelberg and Laura Markowitz.

Introduction

I like to listen. I have learned a great deal from listening carefully. Most people never listen.
Ernest Hemingway

E very so often I wish I were an absolute dictator—an enlightened, benevolent one, of course. Everyone would have to listen to me. Nobody would interrupt me, ever. My smart and dedicated advisors would help me express my ideas and desires, tactfully correct me on the rare occasions when I'm wrong, and never contradict me in public. It would be great!

My fantasy of being heard unconditionally is simply an expression of a universal need: we all want to be heard. Not only that, it would be wonderful to have wise advisors to help us express our nebulous thoughts, give us feedback without making us lose face, and even comfort us during trying times.

As it turns out, the Golden Rule also applies to listening: listening well to others can lead others to listen well to you. So the best way to ensure you will be heard is to become a better listener. I can't help you become a dictator, but I can definitely help you learn to become a better listener. Because listening is so pervasive, even a small improvement will bring tremendous benefits. Listening is the grease that lubricates the engine of communication. Any mechanic will tell you that the time to grease the gears is before it is needed. Without proper listening, the harsh words in an argument grind and grate against one another until the whole communication machine breaks down. Good listening skills and habits will vastly improve the dynamics of your private and business relationships. They will help you satisfy the great human need to be heard. They will earn you genuine respect and admiration, and others will listen to you.

BOOK OVERVIEW

To start things off, Chapter 1 will talk about listening in general. From popular songs to best-selling self-help books to studies and surveys, the importance of listening has been widely trumpeted. What do these general and popular resources have to say about the subject? In addition, how does listening build trust and affirmation? As individuals, why do we care about listening and what are we willing to do to get better at it? Chapter 1 will help you explore and examine the motives for cultivating improved habits of listening.

To get better at something, we have to look at the basics. That's why Chapter 2 will provide an in-depth discussion of listening techniques. Is good listening just a matter of removing distractions, paraphrasing, and asking open-ended questions? What actually are the proper ways to use these techniques, and when do they break down? The important subject of mechanical techniques in listening versus the essence or spirit of listening will also be discussed.

Next, Chapter 3 will discuss empathy. Using women's love of shoes, and other memorable examples, the key aspects of empathy will be explained.

The best techniques in the world, if applied without a clear goal, will just result in a mess. What is the ultimate goal of listening? The purpose of listening really is to serve the speaker's need to speak. Chapter 4 introduces three broad speaking needs and the three corresponding listener roles that satisfy those needs: the Audience, the Contributor, and the Counselor. Chapters 5 through 7 will then discuss each of these three roles in detail.

The hardest time to listen is when you're in an argument. Chapter 8 will talk about real-life situations where it is crucial to remain calm so that you can resolve differences. It will also talk about listening in the business world.

Chapter 9 takes the ideas presented in this book and distills them into an 8-Step Listening Improvement Program. The Program will allow you to apply and gradually hone your listening skills. It is designed to help you build upon your past experience and to give you plenty of opportunities to practice.

Exercise—Self-assessment

The following is a list of things people might say to you if you were a good listener. I call these the Listening Rewards and you will use this in the final chapter to track your listening progress.

How often do people make these statements about you? What habits and practices of yours would prevent people from offering you these praises?

<u>Listening Rewards</u>
I really enjoyed our chat.
You asked good questions. You didn't make me feel stupid.
You made me think. You got me thinking.
You didn't judge. You didn't make me feel bad.
You understood what I was saying.
You allowed me to talk through my different ideas and choices.
Your feedback was very helpful.
You heard my concerns.
I really appreciate your support and encouragement.

————————

WHAT YOU CAN EXPECT

This book is for people who want to use listening to improve their businesses, their career prospects, their marriages, their parenting, and any other interpersonal relationship. Good listening allows you to earn respect and gain influence. If you have been skeptical about listening in the past, I believe you will find answers here. I'm not going to just tell you to "pay attention and listen with your heart" and leave it at that. You should be skeptical about such vague advice. Here, instead, you will find concrete explanations without any jargon. I'm also not just going to point out the various ways people fail to listen. Having a list of common mistakes will not, in itself, help you become a better listener. You also need to know what to aim for and what you need to do correctly.

If you know (or have been told) listening is important, but don't know how to get started, you will find ample exercises in this book to get your listening groove on. The exercises in each chapter will allow you to retrace the steps I took to arrive at my conclusions. They can guide you in expanding your thinking and awareness of listening issues. They also give you a way to personalize the ideas in this book to your own unique situation. Finally, even if you think of yourself as an excellent listener, I still believe this book will make you nod and smile in agreement.

I should also mention something about gender and stereotypes. Among my own limited circle of friends and acquaintances, I have not found men or women to be better or worse listeners. I have not found either men or women to be especially better or worse at helping me talk about my ideas, my fears and frustrations. In fact, until you talk about something more personal or sensitive with someone, it is sometimes quite difficult even to determine who is or isn't a good listener. Society, however, can impart some pretty colorful stereotypes. My view is that people are flexible and can exhibit different kinds of listening behaviors at different times under different circumstances.

Additionally, while some people may be born with artistic and physical talents that allow them to be professional singers or tennis champions, it doesn't mean the average person cannot enjoy music or sports. You don't need to be special to enjoy the process and benefits of listening. Listening, just like singing and tennis, can be fun and social and enjoyed by people at any skill level. More importantly, we can all improve and derive more satisfaction from these activities with a few good tips.

My advice is that you shouldn't let any preconceived notions stop you from learning how to become a better listener. Don't worry about how you were brought up, how you think you should act, how you believe you have always acted since you were three, what your teachers said or didn't say, or what others are going to think. The best way to learn this material is to approach it with a playful, curious mindset. Get feedback. Learn a little bit at a time

WHO AM I?

Now I get to talk about myself. I've always been good at explaining things and I've always been a good listener. But my first exposure to serious listening happened when I volunteered at a telephone crisis center. It was a free service provided to the community and staffed entirely by volunteers. This particular crisis center did not specialize, so to speak. We were not just a suicide prevention line or only a sexual abuse phone line. Callers would call our number to talk about these or any other issue under the sun. A lot of times people would just call to chat.

The volunteers I met there were some of the most amazing people I have had the privilege of knowing. You didn't need to put your guard up when you were talking to a fellow volunteer. You didn't need to worry if they would understand you. Sometimes, you didn't even have to know exactly what you were trying to say; they could help fill in the blanks for you. You could just relax and be yourself around them.

Being a volunteer gives you a chance to encounter some very interesting things. You learn from talking to troubled teens and depressed widows. It is a great privilege to be given the opportunity to listen to a fellow human in need. It is wonderful when you hear that glimmer of hope and relief in the voice of the caller. Your world is forever expanded when the callers are gracious enough to share a part of their sadness and humanity with you. For that, I will always be grateful.

With that, let us get started. As you read this book, think about specifics in your life. Did you encounter similar situations, or opposite situations? Could you have done a better job listening to someone in the past if you'd had the information in this book? And if so, how? Becoming more aware of the richness and sophistication of listening will give you pause the next time you feel the urge to dominate a conversation. By the time you finish this book, you will have a deeper appreciation for listening. You will have better ways to get someone to listen to you, and you will be a better listener.

[I]f you with patient ears attend,
what here shall miss,
our toil shall strive to mend.
William Shakespeare, Prologue to <u>*Romeo and Juliet*</u>

Chapter 1 Why Bother To Listen?

BORE, n. A person who talks when you wish him to listen.
Ambrose Bierce

Why should we bother to listen to people? What's in it for us? Well, in addition to not being a bore, consider this: Sun Tzu, in *The Art of War*, advises that "One can assess advantages through listening."[1] Dale Carnegie devoted an entire chapter in *How to Win Friends and Influence People* to recounting stories about listening, including how he personally listened to others. He recounted stories of customer problems getting resolved by listening. At the end of his chapter, he states: "Be a good listener. Encourage others to talk about themselves."[2]

Stephen Covey, in *7 Habits of Highly Effective People*, lists Habit Five as "Seek First to Understand, Then to Be Understood"[3]. He talks about four developmental stages of empathic listening: mimic content, rephrase content, reflect feeling, rephrase the content and reflect the feeling.

A *New York Times* article on March 13, 2011, titled "Google's Quest to Build a Better Boss,"[4] listed "listen to the issues and concerns of your employees," as a key good behavior of a manager. The article said:

> What employees valued most were even-keeled bosses who made time for one-on-one meetings, who helped people puzzle through problems by asking questions, not dictating answers, and who took an interest in employees' lives and careers.

The Los Angeles Times published an article called "Hey, Doc, Are You Listening?"[5] on July 7, 2011, discussing the importance of listening for doctors. It said:

> When a physician listens respectfully, asks questions and picks up on clues, patients tend to be more involved in their care, more open about what's wrong, and better informed and more satisfied with their visit. Satisfied patients also have fewer hospitalizations, doctor visits and lab tests.

This was followed just days later on July 11, 2011 by another article in *The New York Times* called "New for Aspiring Doctors, the People Skills Test"[6]. It talked about a new interview process used by several medical schools to judge the people skills of incoming students. The article listed two reasons for placing more emphasis on "a pleasant bedside manner and an attentive ear." The first was preventable deaths as a result of poor communications. The second was the increasingly team-based approach to medicine.

Finally, on July 13, 2011, the results of a study commissioned by computer maker Dell, Inc. called

"Listening and Engaging in the Digital Marketing Age,"[7] was released. The accompanying web site[8] stated:

> Companies that launch listening and digital engagement initiatives are rewarded with improved customer satisfaction scores, loyalty and brand metrics, according to a Dell-commissioned research study conducted by Forrester Consulting.

To sum everything up, if you want to win the war, win friends, be effective, be a good manager, improve communications and reduce errors, be a better team player and provide better customer service, then you'd better listen!

In all seriousness, these authors and articles and studies simply confirm what we already know: that listening is important in many facets of life. But what makes it so important? Let's revisit my fantasy for another moment. What if I did manage to become a dictator, except nobody listened to me? I wouldn't be much of a dictator, would I? Without anyone to hear me, I'd be reduced to a crazed lunatic barking orders at the wind. If a tree falls in a forest but no one is there to hear it, does it still make a sound? If I pour my heart out in a forest but no one is there to hear me, do my feelings still count?

Philosophical questions aside, if you tell a joke and nobody laughs, then you know how it feels not to be heard. Of course, your joke or perhaps your delivery might not have been perfect. Nevertheless, your sentiment was not acknowledged or shared. If you think you have a great sense of humor, but your spouse never laughs at your jokes, then you know how frustrating it is never to be heard. You feel unappreciated. The other person doesn't "get" you. You don't feel validated.

As human beings, we want to share our humor and receive laughter. In addition to humor, we want to share our interests with others and receive their affirmation, whether those interests are bowling, online auctions, knitting, sports, whatever. We also want to share our feelings with others. It might be embarrassing if you tell a joke and no one laughs, but it is downright painful and incredibly lonely when you're sad and no one feels your pain. The only way we can share our humor, our thoughts and feelings, our deepest hopes and fears, is if others listen properly. I want to hear your laughter when I tell a funny joke. When I'm upset, I want to know that you understand how frustrated or unhappy I am. If I say something funny or sad without realizing it, I want you to share that with me, too.

Humanistic psychologist Carl R. Rogers had this to say about being truly heard:

> When I have been listened to and when I have been heard, I am able to re-perceive my world in a new way and to go on. It is astonishing how elements that seem insoluble become soluble when someone listens, how confusions that seem irremediable turn into relatively clear flowing streams when one is heard. I have deeply appreciated the times that I have experienced this sensitive, empathic, concentrated listening.[9]

When we listen properly, we affirm and validate that which is communicated. A thought or feeling that is shared is no longer the vague musings and imaginations of a single person. It becomes confirmed by someone other than ourselves. It becomes larger than ourselves. Philosopher Rene Descartes said, "I think, therefore I am."[10] But if he had been contemplating listening, perhaps he would have said: "I listen, therefore *you* are." Listening affirms the speaker's being—his or her thoughts and feelings. Being heard in effect allows the speaker to say, "Someone else appreciates my situation. I'm not the only one that feels that way." This is why listening is so important.

That being said, it is important to note that listening and affirming are not the same as agreeing. Even if I had absolute power, I still wouldn't want to be surrounded by agreeable yes-men looking to stab me in the back at the first opportunity. And as we see from the events making up the Arab Spring, you cannot impose your will on the people forever. You cannot force people to listen and obey forever. The best way for your voice and feelings to be heard is to listen and earn the respect of others first.

At the end of the day, what do you, dear reader, stand to gain or lose by listening? Upon hearing that I was writing a book about listening, a friend of mine immediately responded that he had never been a good listener. He told me he constantly flipped channels when he watched television. He even had picture-in-picture so he could watch two channels at the same time. I thought for a while and then I asked him if when he listened to his clients and his boss, did he change mental channels on them as well? What about you? What personal reasons do you have for listening?

<u>Exercise—What's It to You?</u>

What stereotypes and preconceived notions do you have about listening? Is it hard? Is it simple? Do you know how to do it already? Is it mysterious? Is it for sentimental weaklings only?

Do you prefer to give advice and tell people what to do, or are you more likely to listen and help them find their own answers?

Are you always telling people what they can or can't do, should or shouldn't do?

Do you think you're easy to listen to?

Do you often issue orders to people?

Do you think it is more important to point out people's errors at any cost, or to guide them toward improvement?

What rewards (or punishments) would prompt you to change your listening habits?

What do you hope to gain by listening?

———

TRUST ME, I'M LISTENING

How does listening build trust? We all know that when we talk to others, we take many risks. Just look at the following responses:

"You can't be serious."
"I'm sure it's not that bad."
"I'm sorry, I can't help you."
"I don't understand what you're saying."
"Ha! Excuse me. I didn't mean to laugh."

When we speak to others, our ideas might not be taken seriously. Our concerns might be minimized. Others might not be able or willing to hear or help us. They may not understand us. Worse of all, perhaps, they might laugh at us.

You can offhandedly listen to a child ramble about her day, but you can't do that with someone in the midst of a personal crisis. The more personal, painful, and delicate the subject we wish to discuss, the more we need the listener to respond with respect and sensitivity. Listen well and you will have proven your trustworthiness. This also applies to conflicts. If you're able to respect the differences in a conflict and work toward a constructive resolution, you will have built trust and goodwill. When you build trust and goodwill, you make it easier for others to hear your concerns. By extending a courtesy, you make it much more likely that the favor will be returned.

WHERE TO LEARN?

If listening is so important, then why do we still seem to have so many problems with it? Surveys have shown that therapists overwhelmingly list "Communication" as a top problem among couples[11]. Are we that bad at expressing our wants and desires? Or are we that bad at hearing each other's requests and ideas? Or is it a combination of both?

When we learn about "communication," the emphasis is on writing and public speaking, while the skills of listening and giving helpful or appropriate feedback are not given nearly as much attention.

Consequently, most of us don't have a good way to talk about listening. We tend to lump various hearing activities together and call them all listening. Doing so is as useful as saying the game of golf is just hitting a ball into a hole. Technically, the statement is accurate, but it glosses over the nuances of the game. You can't possibly improve your golf game if you hang on to that simple image. You have to, among other things, learn how to drive the ball and read the green. Similarly, we need a better way to talk about different kinds of listening and a better understanding of the techniques we can employ in different situations.

We tend to think that all feedback is the same. Or we claim that any feedback is better than no feedback. We expect people to be satisfied with our judgments and criticisms. When we do give feedback, we often settle with general observations and fail to be specific.

Also, we typically don't have access to good resources on listening. You can easily turn on the television and watch the best golfers in the world compete against one another. You can easily go to your local driving range or golf course to hit a few rounds. You can easily get lessons to improve your golf game. On the other hand, there aren't that many courses and seminars available to the public that specifically address listening. Maybe one reason is that it doesn't sound cool to say that you want to learn how to listen. I believe that is a perception that must be changed.

In searching for material for this book, I thought perhaps I might find some examples of good listening in movies or novels. But nothing jumped out at me. Perhaps I need to watch more movies and read more books (all in the name of research, of course). But there could be another reason. Dialogues in movies and books are not meant to serve as good examples of listening. They are typically used to advance the plot and to reveal information about the characters. Patient, attentive listening is seldom depicted. Instead dialogue is about the pithy statements characters make to get a laugh or to tell us how they've grown and gained insight or changed. The other problem with looking for examples of good listening in movies and novels is that in fiction, problems by and large get resolved by the end. Life, of course, is not usually this tidy. The story behind a real person's suffering doesn't unfold that neatly.

Television also yielded few examples of good listening. Talk-show hosts are typically charismatic and entertaining, but they are not necessarily good practitioners of selfless listening. A radio or television show has a style, format, and a target audience. A talk show host is primarily interested in ratings. Typically, a talk show will only agree to interview a guest if the guest appeals to the audience in some way. After the host introduces the guest, the guest is given an opportunity to talk. A host wants to get the scoop and make sure there is no dead time or awkward moments during the interview. The guest may be there to comment on something, advocate for a position or policy, reveal something personal or to promote a movie or book or other product. While the host might want the guest to confess unresolved feelings about her latest career move or messy divorce, he's not there to listen deeply and help her come to terms with those feelings. When the time is up, the host breaks for commercial and then moves on to the next story. All this means that popular media and novels are not necessarily good places to go to learn how to listen.

With the advent of social media technologies such as Facebook and Twitter, sharing thoughts and updates about our daily activities has become as simple as clicking a button. Online news articles and blogs invite users to respond, with popular articles collecting hundreds of comments. But has anyone actually become a better listener as a result of all this sharing, updating, and commenting?

As a companion to this book, I have created a website www.8StepListen.com. It is designed as a place for users to practice and improve their listening skills. Virtual conversations—yes, even emails—have many similarities to verbal conversations in their give-and-take. They also have several advantages to auditory listening. For example, you can re-read previous comments; you can take time to compose your responses and edit yourself before you hit Post Comment. I have participated in a number of online conversations, and I usually don't comment unless I feel I have something useful to say. I try to acknowledge the interesting comments others have made before making my own points. Throughout the book, I'll be referring you to the website so you can leverage the 8StepListen user community for knowledge and feedback.

Listening is just one way in which we interact with other people. Learn it for its own sake, because it is such a common and fundamental method of human interaction. The way people speak tells you not just how they see the world, but also what they think about you. Listening is the best way to soak in the thoughts and feelings of those around you. Besides, people—myself included—say the darndest things! If you don't listen, you lose out on all the humor and quirkiness that makes us all unique. If you're still not sure what you can gain by listening, go ahead and ask those around you. Listen to their answers.

THE CORE BENEFITS

Allow me to use a buzz word here. Listening is a tremendous "enabler." At the minimum, we need to coexist with others. Listening allows us to resolve the differences that inevitably occur in human interactions. We are social animals. We need to share our ups and downs with others. We need others to hear us. We accomplish much more when we pool our talent and resources and work toward common goals. Listening makes it possible for us to coordinate those common efforts. Finally, we achieve meaning when we help others by listening.

Now, let us begin our journey on becoming better listeners by taking a look at several important listening skills.

Chapter 2 Listening Skills Reloaded

"I'm listening."
Dr. Frasier Crane (played by *Kelsey Grammer*) on his call-in radio show, from the television sitcom *Frasier*

When we think of experts with listening skills, counselors and therapists come to mind. We imagine a patient lying on a couch next to a box of tissues while the therapist sits off to the side listening passively with clasped hands or jotting down an occasional note. In the movie *Analyze This*, gangster Paul Vitti, played by Robert DeNiro, mocks his therapist, Dr. Sobel, played by Billy Crystal. Paul Vitti says, "This is you: 'Oh, that's interesting. What does that mean to you? Anger is a blocked wish.' "

In popular media, psychologists often ask their patients what they're thinking or what they're feeling. They repeat things their clients have just said. Or they use psychological terms that are mystifying. If you've never spoken to a psychologist, you'd think that those are the only kinds of things they do. In their defense, psychologists are typically highly skilled and trained professionals. They're knowledgeable in many kinds of psychological processes and disorders and they're skilled in various therapeutic techniques and exercises[12].

They're just not always portrayed in a flattering manner. But can listening really be reduced to a set of skills and techniques? How exactly do these techniques work, and when do they fail? The appropriate listening techniques give you the resources and flexibility to achieve your listening goals. The following are a few of the more well-known listening techniques that we'll discuss in this chapter:

Removing distractions and paying attention
Paraphrasing
Asking open-ended questions

PAYING ATTENTION AND A MATTER OF INTEREST

Researchers list four broad types of barriers or noise that interfere with communication: physiological, physical, psychological, and semantic[13]. Physiological barriers refer to your physical being. If you're tired or hungry or sick or had a few drinks, or if you have a headache, it will interfere with your ability to communicate. If the physical surroundings are too hot, too cold, or too noisy, it will also negatively affect communication. Psychological barriers refer to things such as trust and biases and so forth. If you're not honest or truthful or you believe the other side not to be so, it will interfere with communication. If you're angry or overcome with sadness, it will hinder communication. Semantic barriers refer to unclear words or sentences or jargon. Therefore, to facilitate communication, you should make sure both speaker and listener are comfortable and not preoccupied. You should also try to have an open mind about what you're hearing. If the speaker thinks you might be shocked or offended by what he wants to say, he may decide to hold back instead.

In addition to barriers, you must also pay attention to how the speaker looks and acts. Is she hesitating? Is she pausing with a look of consternation on her face? Is she shifting around uneasily in her chair? Does her body language match the words she's saying, or is there a discrepancy that warrants further investigation? Is her voice tense or is she acting nervous? Paying attention to a speaker is like looking for "tells" during a poker game. A poker tell is a poker player's unconscious reaction to the good or bad cards being dealt and to the ongoing game play. Tells can reveal information useful to other players. Wikipedia states that:

> Some possible tells include leaning forward or back, placing chips with more or less force, fidgeting, doing chip tricks, or making any changes in one's breathing, tone of voice, facial expressions, direction of gaze or in one's actions with the cards, chips, cigarettes or drinks.[14]

Of course, listening is not a competitive game where participants bluff and quit in the middle of a round by folding. The speaker is not your opponent and the purpose of good observation in listening is not to outwit him or her. But the analogy is still useful for training yourself to become a better listener. For example, in poker, it isn't just a matter of noting that one player bet a dollar and another raised the bet by two dollars. How each player places his bets can also be important.

"I bet one dollar," he said a bit too casually.

"I bet one dollar," she said aggressively.

When you hear someone say, "I feel sad," you also need to pay attention to the way it was said.

"I feel sad," he said a bit too casually.

"I feel sad," she said aggressively.

In addition, how is the speaker reacting wittingly or unwittingly to his story and to the ongoing conversation? What non-verbal signals is he sending? Did his breathing change when he talked about his wife? Is he looking at his feet when he talks about his father, or does he glance around the room or stare off into the distance?

Playing poker also requires putting on a "poker face"—an attempt to reveal as little information to other players as possible. But when you listen, you're not trying to hide or suppress your own reactions. Instead, you want to be aware of anything you're doing that might interfere with the other person's willingness to speak freely. What signals are you sending, consciously and unconsciously? Some are more obvious. If you find you can't stop yourself from checking your watch or email, then perhaps you should be honest with the speaker and let him know you're preoccupied with something else. If you find yourself yawning despite your best efforts to stay focused, then you may simply be too tired or uninterested. Your reactions might also be a bit more subtle. Did you tense up because you heard something you didn't like? Did you start tapping your feet or your pen impatiently as you listened to a story you'd already heard twice before? Either ask the speaker to clarify the significance of the discussion or take a coffee break, or even reschedule altogether. If you're offended or find yourself wincing or violently disapproving, then you might wish to excuse yourself politely from the discussion.

Additionally, just as a poker player has to think about the logic of the game, the listener has to think about the logic of the story she is listening to. A poker player thinks about her chances of getting a good hand. A good listener thinks about the plot of the story she is listening to. Who is the good guy? Who is the bad guy? What is the conflict? Good observation and analysis allows a poker player to recall an opponent's behavior in a previous hand quite easily. The poker player not only saw how her opponent played out his hand, but she thought about the reasons why her opponent would do so. The good listener thinks about why the speaker acted the way he did in the story he's telling. Good observation and analysis allows a listener to concentrate on the important elements of what she is hearing, and to remember significant points.

A good listener pays as much attention to the speaker as a good poker player does at the gambling table. She observes the body language of the speaker, looks for clues that might reveal the emotional state of the speaker, and is aware of her own physical reactions and emotional state. A good listener is present and attentive to the entire conversation, and is open to both the speaker's and her own presence and experience, while thinking critically about the story or issue being discussed. Being "there", "present", "in tune with," and "on the same wavelength" are some of the ways we describe this state of awareness. At the end of a good poker game (or sports event or movie, for that matter), you feel mentally alert, and you can recall highlights in delicious detail. At the end of a good conversation, you feel mentally alert, perhaps a little tired as well, and you can recall highlights in vivid detail. Paying this kind of attention and having these reactions is one way you know you have truly listened to and engaged with the speaker.

Now, before you all run out and use this as an excuse for playing more poker, may I remind you that the opposite argument can also be made. Call me crazy, but I'll bet your spouse will want you to spend more time listening and improving your observational and self-awareness skills before you head off to your poker game.

On the other hand, if you're the one doing the talking and you find that your listener seems distracted, feel free to confirm with him that it's a good time to talk. If the listener doesn't seem to be as engaged or present as he should be, pause for a moment. Feel free to reiterate the significance of the information you're trying to relay. Feel free to email more background information and come back later to resume the discussion. In other words, be more aware of whether both of you are paying attention or losing interest, and look for ways to correct the situation.

Note also that casinos are not completely free of noise and distractions, yet poker players manage to stay focused on the game. Likewise, we can all remember good jokes or stories we heard at parties or at noisy bars. If you were engrossed or captivated, you might even remember what hors d'oeuvres you were eating as you listened, and be able to vividly recall the moment someone bumped your elbow and you almost spilled a drink. If you were engaged in the moment, you easily can recall the story as well as information about yourself and the environment. Our ability to focus, even under non-ideal conditions, is driven naturally by our curiosity and desire to understand, and by the emotional impact of the event. Poker players don't have to go through a laundry list to remind themselves how to pay attention at the card table, just as party-goers don't need to remind themselves how to listen to good stories when they are socializing.

Exercise—Distract Me

Have a friend help you with this. First, think of something you find interesting. Then talk to your friend about it. Ask your friend randomly to do one of the following while you're talking:

Scratch his head
Look at his watch
Clear his throat
Check his cell phone
Yawn
Lift his hand to cover his eyes

Did you notice when it happened? How did it feel? Now repeat the exercise. But this time, when you see your friend getting distracted, try to come up with a question to bring the conversation back on track. For example:

"Are you tired?"
"Do you need a break?"
"Is something wrong?"
"Do you need to do something?"

Be careful not to use accusatory questions or statements, which tend to make people angry or defensive, or both. For example:

"Did you hear what I said?"
"Are you paying attention?"
"Hey! Wake up!"

Can you list other accusatory questions or statements?

———

SHOWING INTEREST

Most of us have no problem paying attention to good movies and favorite television shows. We drop everything to check out the latest viral Internet video. We're interested. We want to know the outcome. On the other hand, if the topic is something we find boring or uninteresting, you'd have to pay us to watch it. Our desire to listen is also largely determined by our level of interest. If we're interested, it's a breeze to listen. Furthermore, it's usually more pleasant to listen to a fun story rather than a sad story. It's often more pleasant to listen to a story of excitement instead of a story of frustration. But if we're not interested in something, then good luck getting us to listen!

Exercise—What Makes Them Tick?

What are some things that your family members like to talk about that don't interest you?

What are some things that people at work like to talk about that you're not interested in, or that makes you frustrated to hear?

What are some things that you wish your family members would be more interested in hearing you speak about?

Why is there a lack of mutual interest?

———

An important part of holding a listener's interest is to keep her in the loop. When people get news out of the blue, they feel surprised and caught off guard. Your listener might need time to catch up. "I didn't realize we were so far behind on that! Why didn't you tell me sooner?" Or she might even demand an explanation for why she was not informed earlier. Make sure employees, managers, customers and family members are informed of significant events. For example, if you want your father to buy you a skateboard, you might approach it this way:

"Dad, you know how I've been practicing hard? I want to take it to the next level. I'd like some money to buy a better skateboard."

Keeping people informed seems like common sense or common courtesy. But when we feel our managers are a pain, our spouses are too critical, our parents too out of touch, our customers too demanding, then we stop communicating to avoid the hassle. In these cases, try to get to the bottom of the problem and resolve it so that we feel heard and we can hear others.

In some cases you might want to make a bargain by sharing interests with each other. "I'll go along with ballroom dancing if you go with me to football games." Even better, help the other person appreciate your interests or understand your point of view by sharing your enthusiasm and expertise on the topic. For example, what are the current rivalries in tennis? What are the latest developments in digital photography? You can make it fun for them to develop an interest in your passions. Try relating your hobby with an interest of theirs. "You like to cook and I love to take photographs. Why don't you make a complicated recipe and I will take pictures and we can post them on our Facebook page." Don't expect your spouse to become an instant expert. But who knows? You might discover that you both like similar things, as in the famous song "Escape" by Rupert Holmes[15].

Ultimately, however, there are still going to be areas about which you disagree or have no compelling interest. No two people can agree on everything. Even deciding what should be a priority and what is no big deal can shut down constructive communication. I remember one occasion when I was in a client's office and the phone rang. It was my client's wife calling to remind him to bring home supplies for their son's birthday party. My client was a little exasperated. "My son's one year old! He doesn't even know what's going on!" But the birthday party was most likely important for the mother, who was anxious about the cake and the treats and the success of the party. The birthday party may have been an opportunity for the parents in the neighborhood to get together to celebrate a milestone in the child's life and the whole family's life. Therefore, it would reflect badly on the mother if the guests were not fed and entertained and made comfortable in every reasonable way. The mother would quite understandably feel pressure to get everything done right, which meant she would pass some of that pressure on to the father.

Society has many roles and expectations of individuals that can be difficult to avoid or resist. If a child is not well dressed, we're more likely to blame the mother than the father. If a dinner party is not successful, we're more likely to blame the hostess instead of the host. If a man drives an old, beat-up car, we tend to think he's either cheap or poor. If a little boy doesn't know how to play sports, we tend to blame the father. The best thing to do in these cases is for both parties to try to acknowledge that the problem stems from different, and possibly conflicting, priorities. Try to discuss these potential flash points as early as possible, before arguments happen. What are your expectations for household cleanliness? How should money be spent? How should children be disciplined? What about sex? There are no right or wrong answers, and listening carefully to the other's point of view and feeling heard in return is a valuable experience. When issues inevitably come up, try to appreciate each other's reasons, compromise, and do a little give and take. If all else fails, agree to disagree.

Exercise—What Makes Them Tick, Part 2

List topics about which you and those around you hold different priorities. For example:

Peer acceptance for teenagers, wearing the "right" clothes, going to the "right" parties, etc.

Playing video games

Watching sports

In-laws

Independence versus safety for children and teenagers

Holidays, anniversaries, celebrations and other traditions

Household cleanliness

Sex

Profits

Customer service

Recycling and eco-friendliness

How to spend money

What is important to you?

———

Do You Understand Me?

When you're writing a research paper and you need to reference original material, you have to follow the appropriate citation guidelines to quote, paraphrase and summarize. When you listen to someone, you can repeat back what they've said in order to clarify something. You can also paraphrase what they've said.

Merriam-Webster defines "paraphrase" as:

"a restatement of a text, passage, or work giving the meaning in another form."

Consider the following examples:

ORIGINAL: I'm worried about my job.
PARAPHRASE: I might get fired.
ORIGINAL: We had a computer security breach.
PARAPHRASE: Some hackers got into our computer systems.

ORIGINAL: The judge handed down an unfavorable decision.
PARAPHRASE: We lost the court case.

Paraphrasing can be very useful in confirming we understood something. It can also be used to put things in more straightforward terms by clarifying jargon or indirect language.

Merriam-Webster defines "summary" as:

"COMPREHENSIVE; *especially*: covering the main points succinctly"

In addition to paraphrasing and summarizing, it is useful to think about "generalizing." Merriam-Webster defines "generalize" as:

"to derive or induce (a general conception or principle) from particulars."

To illustrate these points, let us look at an example. I was having lunch with a couple of friends when I noticed something odd in my salad.

"It's just a piece of ginger," said Shirley.

I carefully pushed the object to the side of my plate.

"That looks like a complimentary protein supplement to me," I said skeptically. "Besides, ginger doesn't have limbs."

Bill leaned in to get a closer look.

"Ginger doesn't have legs!" he laughed.

Bill obviously got the joke. Bill was paraphrasing here. If he had said, "Ginger doesn't have hair," it would not be paraphrasing and it might have taken the conversation in a slightly different direction. Plus, I might not be as squeamish about hair.

"Or wings!" he continued.

"Yeah, we get it!" says Shirley. "Ginger doesn't have insect parts."

Bill and I are laughing like little kids at this point. Shirley was summarizing here, stopping Bill from listing all the insect parts that ginger doesn't have. We all looked a little closer. As it turns out, it was indeed a piece of ginger.

"I just don't like suspicious looking things in my salad," I concluded, generalizing about salads to excuse my false alarm.

As you can see, paraphrasing, summarizing and generalizing can be very useful. You can use them when you're writing research papers, when you're talking about computer security, court cases, and foreign objects in food! It is clear that these techniques are fairly commonplace. By laughing, Bill showed outward signs that he understood and appreciated the joke. By paraphrasing, he demonstrated it conclusively. Paraphrasing is a highly effective way of confirming that you understand someone.

You can paraphrase when there's a lull in the conversation. In effect, you're saying, "Yes, I agree. Please continue." You can paraphrase when the speaker is hesitating or repeating himself as if he's trying to make sure you understand. You can also paraphrase if the speaker says any of the following:

"Do you know what I mean?"

"How else can I say it?"

In addition, by paraphrasing, Bill also participated in and shared in the joke. Shirley, on the other hand, used summarizing to stop Bill from continuing down that conversational track. As the dictionary definition above explains, a summary can be comprehensive. If someone makes several statements and you're able to sum them up in a comprehensive fashion, then you have completed the thought. Summarizing can be used not just to confirm that you understood the speaker, but to broaden the scope of the topic. Shirley was also able to participate in the joke. And in my concluding remark about salads, I used generalizing to express an overall sentiment.

Applying these ideas to emotions, when a friend tells you something is troubling him and you sigh, you are showing that you understand his frustration. When you accurately paraphrase his concerns, you demonstrate intellectually and verbally that you hear him. You demonstrate it conclusively. If you can summarize his feelings, that means you can make a comprehensive statement about it. If you can generalize his thoughts, then it means you have inferred something from what he has told you.

But things can go wrong. Everyone knows that it isn't always easy to re-tell a joke. A joke, or a sentiment, or a feeling, can be very hard to capture. A joke dies if you mess up the punch line or get the timing wrong. Just as we know when someone isn't doing a good job re-telling a joke, we can also easily tell when someone does a poor job reflecting an emotion back to the speaker. We can feel it. When that happens, it sounds insincere. Doing a poor job is one thing, but faking it is worse.

In addition, the listener has to acknowledge the implications of what the speaker is saying within the overall context of the situation, especially if it's an urgent one.

"I can't find the tickets."

"We're late already. Did you check your wallet?"

A straight paraphrase here can actually make you sound mean or sarcastic. "You're saying you can't locate the tickets."

If you're sympathetic to the speaker and you use the tools of paraphrasing, summarizing and generalizing well, they are very effective. But if you force yourself to do it, when you don't understand or appreciate what the speaker is saying or going through, then you're just patronizing the speaker. You appear insensitive and insincere. There is much more to showing you understand a speaker than coming up with synonyms. Done badly, you end up sounding sarcastic or like a jerk who never got the joke in the first place. This is why it's easy to parody incompetent listeners. Just paraphrase something poorly and we immediately recognize that the listener never understood the speaker in the first place. With summarizing and generalizing, there is also an additional risk that you have taken meanings too far or gone in the wrong direction. So be sure to check back with the speaker to see if you are on target.

In addition, it isn't mandatory that you paraphrase or summarize or generalize. You can use opposite and complementary concepts to show that you understood someone.

"The results are up in the air," said one.

"At least your plan was down to earth," replied the other.

"I'm interested in teaching," said one.

"Great! I'm interested in learning," replied the other.

You can use these various language techniques for different listening goals. By themselves, they are neutral. In fact, in the salad example above, Shirley used summarization to stop Bill. These language techniques can be used just as easily to validate feelings or to show disapproval. They can also be overused. You cannot reword everything someone says in a conversation, or keep saying, "I understand." People get bored or even annoyed if you overuse or misuse words and language devices. The key to not offending someone when you're paraphrasing them is to be honest about how you feel. Make sure you understand the joke or feel sympathetic toward the speaker's concerns. If you don't, then ask the speaker to clarify. Make sure you think about the implications of what you're hearing. If you still don't understand or you feel there is a fundamental disagreement, then you should let the speaker know that you might not be the most appropriate audience for that particular issue. In the long run, you cannot quote, paraphrase, summarize and generalize your way out of genuine sympathy and concern.

Exercise—"You Can't Handle the Truth!"
Here's a fun exercise that you can try alone or with others. Try to paraphrase your favorite movie

quotes. For example, in the 1992 movie *A Few Good Men*, Colonel Jessup (played by Jack Nicholson) is cross-examined and challenged in court by Lieutenant Daniel Kaffee (played by Tom Cruise). In response, Jessop thunders the memorable line, "You can't handle the truth!" How do you feel about the following alternatives:

"You can't handle reality!"

"You don't appreciate the life-threatening circumstances we face and you don't respect the unpleasant choices we are forced to make!"

You can take further inspiration from the American Film Institute's *AFI's 100 Years...100 Movie Quotes*. Don't worry about being as pithy or concise as the original. Are some quotes easier to paraphrase than others? Why? How does it feel to paraphrase something? Does it help to be "in character" when you're paraphrasing? Why do you think it is fun to paraphrase movie quotes?

What technical terms and jargon have you come across in your work? How would you rephrase those words to clarify meaning to customers or management?

Next, try to summarize or generalize your favorite movie quotes. Describe the implications of those quotes. For example, you might generalize Jessup's statement as follows: "People who haven't served on the frontline aren't capable of handling the reality of our nation's security!" And the implication of the statement might be: "I will make you pay for your disrespect!"

―――――

The improper use of terminology has a similar effect as bad paraphrasing. If you misuse technical terms, you appear incompetent. For example, if you call the five common cards in Texas Hold'em "public cards" instead of "community cards", people will immediately think you're an amateur. Make sure you understand the technical terms used in your field. Learn the proper way to talk about processes in your field. Learn the new things that are impacting or changing your industry, and use the right terms to describe them.

OPEN-ENDED AND OTHER TYPES OF QUESTIONS

I keep six honest serving-men
(They taught me all I knew);
Their names are What and Why and When
And How and Where and Who.
Rudyard Kipling

Any doctor will tell you that asking the right question can literally be a matter of life and death. Lawyers will tell you that asking the right questions in court can be the difference between freedom and imprisonment. Scientists will tell you that the right questions can lead to the most startling breakthroughs and discoveries. Perhaps most importantly, teachers will tell you that the right questions can open doors to new ideas and whole new ways of thinking.

When someone asks a good question, you know they have listened. Good questions show that you have heard and thought about the content. You're not just passively absorbing what is being said. You're thinking about it, then forming your own ideas and questions based on what you've heard. I once did some work with a client. We had a couple of status meetings at key points during the project. I provided updates on the project and also bought up different issues for discussion. What I remember most from those meetings were the intelligent and thoughtful questions asked by one of the managers. He would hone in on the most relevant solution and ask, "You mentioned an option in your presentation. What are the costs and benefits of that option?" I never felt his questions were mean or designed to make my presentations look lacking. They allowed me to elaborate on certain points and emphasize specific details. His questions kept me on my toes and I always looked forward to them.

Let's begin our look at the types of questions we can ask. Journalists have used "What, why, when, how, where, and who" for years to guide them in writing their stories. A story is considered complete if it answers all these questions. Our purpose as listeners, however, is a little different. We use questions to help the speaker to discover the key points of his or her story. What is the problem (or the cause for celebration)? What are they upset or worried about? Why are they upset about it? When did it start to bother them? How did it happen? Where did it take place? Who is involved in this?

One advantage of these questions is that they are open-ended. An open-ended question is a question that doesn't lend itself to a yes or no answer, but rather encourages a more detailed response. The following are some examples of closed and open-ended questions:

Closed questions:
"Did you get a raise?"
"Did you like the movie?"
"Is that a new shirt?"

Open-ended questions:
"What happened at the meeting with your boss?"
"What did you like about the movie?"
"Where did you buy that shirt?"

Besides journalistic questions, you can also use questions to clarify what someone is implying. If your friend says, "Well, isn't it convenient how that worked out!" in a sarcastic tone, you can say, "Do you think this is rigged or unfair in some way?" If your friend is unusually silent or makes a face, you might ask, "Do you have any concerns or reservations about this?" Use these questions to encourage people to voice their concerns. On the other hand, if you ask these questions in an aggressive manner, then you're just silencing people, as if you're challenging them: "You have something to say!?"

Questions can be used to discover the scope of an event or situation. For example:

"We canceled the holiday party for budget reasons."

"Really? What else are they cutting? Are you still going to have a bonus this year? Are they going to start firing people?"

The purpose here is to allow the speaker to elaborate on the scope. If the speaker wasn't your friend talking about her company, but one of your co-workers talking about yours, you might react with much more panic and concern. That is because your own interests would be threatened. On the other hand, if you don't work there, you might not care as much about budget cuts at your friend's company.

Questions can also be used gently to check assumptions and refocus our attention:

"Why are you trying to solve so many problems at once?"

"Why are you so upset about your co-workers?"

"Why is this so important to you?"

"Why do you expect this optimistic or unfavorable outcome?"

"Why is going to the concert so important to you?"

"Why are you being so hard on yourself?"

"Why are you being so hard on everyone else?"

These questions are useful when someone seems to be overly anxious, critical or excited about something. You're asking the speaker to consider whether their agitation is proportional to the significance of the underlying event. Maybe it is. Maybe it deserves even more attention! Maybe there just needs to be an agreed upon plan with a time-table and intermediate goals to bring better organization to the task at hand. Maybe there are good reasons for you to be supportive and you just needed to give the speaker a chance to tell you.

Questions can be used to help us examine our motives or goals:

"What is the point of working so many hours that you never see your family?"

"Do you really think your current actions will solve the problem, or are you just retaliating or venting your frustration?"

"Do you really want what's best for your children, or are you more concerned that they will make the same mistakes you did?"

"Are you trying to make someone be nice to you?"

"Are you trying to make a sale or help a customer?"

"Are you trying to make someone give you what you want?"

Questions can be used to help your friend understand why something is bothering her and to find out what she can do about it. Imagine your friend tells you that her boyfriend is always flirting with other women. You can come right out and ask your friend to pick between two alternatives:

"Is he just friendly or do you feel he enjoys women's attention a little too much for your comfort? Does he like to flirt in general? What exactly does he do?"

This leads to a few follow-up questions:

"Are there any other warning signs that he might be cheating? Is he generally dedicated and devoted to his relationship with you? What do you think he should do to reassure you? What would you like to see happen?"

In other words, is there a straightforward explanation for what is happening or is there something more going on? What further information is there that might shed light on the situation? Is there a better way to determine the severity of the situation? What, ideally, would the speaker like to see happen?

In order to come up with questions to ask the speaker, you can ask yourself, "What would I do if the problem happened to me? What if my boyfriend flirted with other people?" Things take on more immediacy and meaning when we imagine our own welfare is at stake.

If that still doesn't do the trick and clear up confusion, then imagine a similar situation, or a more extreme one. "What if your boyfriend pinched attractive women?" In that case, it might be more obvious that his actions are inappropriate and insensitive. They're inappropriate to the person being mistreated, and insensitive to the girlfriend who has to watch this happen. Does this assessment then apply to your friend's original problem about her boyfriend's flirting? What's the solution to the similar or more extreme case? Imagining a similar or worse situation helps us to see the caveats and the considerations of our current situation more clearly. Can the solution to the imagined situation then be used to solve the original problem?

In some cases, we're guilty of double standards. We'd like others to do more than we, ourselves, are willing to do. If your friend thinks his wife shouldn't have spent money on something, you might ask:
"What if you wanted to buy something?"
What if the tables were turned around? Is it okay for him to lie to his kids or his subordinates? Is it okay for his kids or his subordinates to lie to him? What kinds of things did he do when he was younger? What trouble did he get into? What kinds of things does he not want to tell his spouse?

If someone seems stuck in a situation, there are a series of exploratory questions that can help him or her examine expectations and think about what to do next. For example, the following questions can be asked if there is a disagreement or an unsatisfactory situation at home or in the office:
"What do you think will happen if you don't change things?"

"Do you expect the situation to change? If so, when?"

"What would prompt you to try something different to resolve the issue? Do you really want to wait for that to happen? Has it already happened?"

"What's the worse that would happen if you made a change?"

"What are the benefits of making a change?"

"What are the costs of making a change?"

"What exactly are we trying to do or fix here?"

"If we use this fix, will it cause problems elsewhere?"

"What do you think is the right thing to do?"

"What would make the current situation more acceptable to you? Is there a way to make that happen?"

"Is there a way for everyone to win?"

By asking these questions, you're trying to get the speaker to entertain different possibilities and to understand the options. You might even want to brainstorm some ideas. You want to concentrate on the positive and getting things done right. The quickest or most convenient or most superficially painless solutions may be tempting, but they don't always last and often have other costs. Try to avoid options where one party wins and the other party loses. Resist the urge to rule out good solutions that might require some short-term sacrifice. Look for long-term solutions where everyone can gain something.

When faced with a problem that doesn't seem to have any answers, it can be useful to start with broad questions and to gradually narrow things down. "What is the worst-case scenario? What is the best-case scenario?" These questions can help put a limit on the range of possibilities that have to be considered. If the worst case is indeed dire, such as a company going bankrupt and laying off all the workers, then what is the likelihood of that happening? What are further signs that the company is headed down that path? And what can be done to stop it or prepare for it? How likely is the best-case scenario? What actions can be taken to enhance the probability that it will happen? In addition to the best and worst cases, is there a most-likely scenario?

Exercise—Go Ahead, Ask Me!

Think about as many current or past situations as you can where there was some confusion. What kind of questions might have helped clarify things?

Think of an ambiguous situation at work or at home. What would you do under a similar or worse situation?

What questions would you ask to determine the scope of an event or the implications of a situation?

A friend asks you, "Should I quit my job and go back to school?" What questions would you ask to help them explore the reasons and feasibility of such an undertaking?

Look at your favorite advice column. Instead of giving advice, what questions would you use to help someone sound out their thoughts and concerns and perhaps arrive at their own solution?

Go to the Forum section of my website www.8StepListen.com and review the topic "Practice asking good questions". Here, you can practice asking questions, vote on other people's responses and even submit your own scenarios. See what helpful questions the community is able to generate.

––––––––

We all have uncomfortable questions that we'd rather not answer. We certainly don't want to be forced to answer personal questions under a spotlight. I'm also not saying you should ask questions to show off how smart you are, or to show that you have done your research. Those are good things, but they don't necessarily prove that you have listened. The point of all this is to examine why things are the way they are and what can be done to change it for the better. It isn't important for the listener to supply the answers. There may not even be any answers, but just thinking about the questions might lead to some interesting results. And the results don't have to be spoken. As listeners, we're not trying to interrogate or cross-examine. Our purpose isn't to challenge people or to find fault. We're not conducting an interview either, or trying to uncover juicy nuggets for our own amusement. We're simply using questions to help the speaker to explore and understand his or her unique situation. Whether the speaker shares any resulting thoughts and feelings is entirely up to him or her.

ART VERSUS TECHNIQUE

Listening is an art. As an art form, it resembles movie making in some very interesting ways. Generally speaking, a movie can entertain, inform, inspire or touch an audience. With good listening, it is the *speaker* who is entertained, informed, inspired or touched. In a movie, the story has to resonate with the viewers. The movie-making magic is used to tell the human story. Your listening has to reach the speaker, or perhaps more accurately, to allow the speaker to reach *him or herself.* This is the spirit, the goal of listening. In fact, you want to help the speaker talk out his emotions even if his ideas are not well-formed, his arguments are not crystal clear, or his feelings are hurt. You want the speaker to feel good, maybe even relieved, after he's spoken to you. You're there to help the speaker tell his story, to share his excitement or displeasure, to discover the meaning or truth, if there is any, behind his confusion or suffering.

Movie makers have to take care of costumes, lighting, special effects, and a variety of other elements. Sloppy movies distract the viewer from the story at hand. Visual gaffes and discontinuities wake the viewer from any suspense of disbelief. Instead of enjoying the moment in the movie, I notice that a Roman gladiator is wearing a digital watch. If the errors continue, I end up spending more time looking for them rather than following the story. I become completely distracted. Poor listening prevents the speaker from immersing herself in *her* own story. Instead of being able to feed off genuine interest and shared reactions with the listener, the speaker notices that you're not "with her". If I'm talking about video games and you somehow signal to me that you're not interested, then I don't want to bore you with the details. If you don't understand my frustration, I don't want to keep talking about my problems. Or worse, if you interrupt me or minimize my concerns, then I feel even more frustrated. In general, if you don't listen to me the right way, I can't whole-heartedly engage in my story and express my true feelings about it. Poor listening techniques or habits distract the speaker.

Finally, repeated and overused storylines in movies can also fail to capture the viewer's imagination. Boy meets girl, boy loses girl, boy wins girl back. The same story gets tiring after a while. Even good listening techniques, when used in a formulaic and predictable manner, might prompt the speaker to question the sincerity and interest of the listener. Your problems may be universal, but they are personal and have specific meaning to you. We don't want our unique experiences to be listened to by someone who is only going through the motions.

Exercise—Photos Versus Memories

There are many areas in life where the emotional response or attachment is more important than the techniques used to create them. There are many commercial products and services where the value is greater than the sum of its parts. Childhood memories give old toys their sentimental value. A good story is better than good grammar and punctuation. The irreplaceable family photos are priceless to you and nobody else because of the memories associated with them. Athletes entertain and inspire. A luxury car is more than a means of transportation. How are your hobbies and interests more than just a pastime? How is your work or your company's product greater than the sum of its parts?

———

THE RESPONSIBLE LISTENER

It is the province of knowledge to speak and it is the privilege of wisdom to listen.
Oliver Wendell Holmes

If you are genuinely interested in someone else's opinion and feelings, you will not find it difficult to focus on what they are saying. During the course of the conversation, there will be natural opportunities for you to confirm your understanding by paraphrasing the speaker. There will be moments when it is appropriate to summarize what has been discussed or to generalize what has been said. It will not be difficult to find questions that encourage the speaker to think things through and to express her or his thoughts. If you are listening for the right reasons, with the right frame of mind, you will have some good ideas as to how to proceed and how to behave. You will notice the speaker crossing his arms and withdrawing. You will know when to lean forward and use a soft voice. You will know what to do to put people at ease and to allow people to talk.

However, if you force the use of listening techniques simply because you read about them somewhere, your actions will appear insincere and contrived. Imagine the following dialogue:

"Daddy, why are you crying?" asks a little girl in a soft voice. Daddy wipes his tears but doesn't answer.

The little girl leaves the room and returns moments later.

"When I'm unhappy, I like to hold onto Mr. Brown," she says, handing her father a well-worn teddy bear.

When it comes down to it, you can use the simplest words and actions to convey your sincere sympathy and genuine desire to help. In fact, no technique can replace that. The little girl wants to know what is troubling her father, but never pushes for an answer. And even though she is never given an answer, she is still willing to hand over her most cherished possession to comfort her father. She knows she cannot solve her father's problems, but she does not let that stop her from caring and offering comfort. She doesn't know the exact reasons for her father's tears, but she recognizes and responds to the sadness. The little girl's actions don't make her weak. In fact, she is the one in this picture with poise and presence. She isn't embarrassed by her father's tears. She doesn't look down on him for becoming emotional.

Of course, a little girl has certain advantages because of her innocence. She is not expected to have any ulterior motives. She might be more trustworthy because she will not tell her friends about all the bad things happening at home. But she also has some disadvantages. A little girl is not expected to understand the complexities of adult life. She doesn't have the vocabulary or the experience to discuss adult themes. As a good listener, you have to earn the trust of the speaker. Your desire to help and your motivations for helping should be as pure as the little girl's. You use all the tools for the selfless purpose of helping the speaker. Even if you know the answers, you don't just tell people what to do. You accept people's pain and you don't judge it. You help people calm down first and then you help them find their own answers. If you're not able to help, for whatever reason, you admit it frankly. Finally, like the little girl, you give people the best that you can offer.

<u>Exercise—It's Not the Size That Matters</u>
Can you think of any small actions that convey sincere sympathy and a genuine desire to help?

SUMMARY

In summary, pay attention and engage in the conversation. Observe the speaker and also be aware of your own reactions to the conversation. You may not be interested in listening for a wide variety of reasons. Whenever possible, try to anticipate differences ahead of time. If this cannot be done, then try to acknowledge that the issue has different levels of significance to each party and work toward a compromise. Failing that, agree to disagree.

Tools such as paraphrasing, summarizing, and generalizing allow you intellectually and verbally to confirm that you understand a speaker and also to participate in a conversation. They are by no means a substitute for understanding and sympathy.

Use questions to help other people understand the issues they are facing. What is the beginning, middle, and end of their story? Who are the players? Use questions to keep a conversation on track, to clarify confusion, to resolve conflicting information and so on.

You can use questions to explore possibilities, to encourage thinking and understanding, and to find ways to make things better.

Listening techniques are the tools that allow you to help the speaker express his or her own story and delve deeper. At the end of the day, it is your honest and selfless desire to help that should drive the use of any technique. But please remember that you can't use a technique to mask indifference, silent judgment, hidden agendas, or carelessness.

With a thorough understanding of listening techniques, you can clear up misconceptions and diagnose problems. You can set clear goals for improvement.

Chapter 3 Well-Heeled Empathy

"Rather than pointing fingers or assigning blame, let us use this occasion to expand our moral imaginations, to listen to each other more carefully, to sharpen our instincts for empathy, and remind ourselves of all the ways our hopes and dreams are bound together."
Barack Obama, at the memorial service after the Tucson shootings in 2011

E mpathy is critical to good listening. It is the ability to appreciate what someone else is going through without actually experiencing the triggering event. At the core of empathy is understanding. Specifically, understanding the various reasons why people do different things. The first part of the chapter will review some general challenges people face at different stages of life. Next, we'll look at specific cases of empathy. We'll extract insights from the simplest cases to something much more complicated: women's shoes!

SEVEN AGES

Shakespeare wrote about the Seven Ages of Man in *As You Like It*: "And one man in his time plays many parts, his acts being seven ages."[16] Man goes from being a helpless infant, a lover, a soldier, a middle-aged man, back to being a helpless old man and dying. No matter who you are, no matter what you do, life is tough. As a small child, you cannot do whatever you want to do. You cannot go wherever you want to go. You have to learn that hitting people, taking their toys, and temper tantrums are bad. In school, you're constantly compared with other children. At home, you're constantly compared with your siblings. As a teenager, you struggle with figuring out who you are and how you fit in. You need to transition from the little child's black and white fairy-tale world to the gray adult world of compromises and sacrifices. You want more freedom to have fun and you hate being treated like a child. You watch your parents fight and you rebel by acting out. Perhaps, like J.D. Salinger's Holden Caulfield[17], you feel that people are all "phonies." As a young adult, you have no money and you don't know where your career and life will take you. You just plan to get by, or you might have wild dreams of success. Life is full of possibilities, if only you can get a decent job and find the time to enjoy it. You stick to your ideals and you get into violent fights with your bosses and your lovers. You might even get your first divorce. As a middle-aged person, you worry about your mortgage, your children and your aging parents. You try not to think about the abuse from your boss. You think that makes you a responsible adult. You might even be okay with the things that should or should not have happened to you as a child. Your youthful dreams are either long forgotten or you try to relive your past through toys and reckless adventures. But your body cannot do what it could before. As an old person, you worry about diet and exercise. You still wish things were like the good, old, simple days. You talk to your friends about cholesterol drugs and blood-thinners. In the end, you might get to live out a few relatively pain-free years and go peacefully in your sleep.

Sounds rough, doesn't it? But wait, there's more! That was just some of the challenges based on what stage of life you are at. There are gender-based difficulties as well. As a woman, you worry about how you look. You worry about how the house looks. You worry about your loved ones. You worry about being passed over a promotion by the all-male management team. You wish your husband would understand you. As a man, you worry about whether you're manly enough. You worry about being successful, beating the other guy. You think about sex all the time. You want to be left alone either to read the paper or to watch the game. You don't want drama. You don't want to deal with that vague and confusing emotional stuff. You don't want to be forced to guess what is on your wife's mind and be punished for guessing wrong.

Different personalities also face different challenges. A character strength in one situation can easily become a weakness in another. Perseverance in one situation can turn into stubbornness in another. An outgoing personality may be good in some situations, but inappropriate in others. Easy-going people are great to work with, but are occasionally not assertive enough. Intelligent people can be stubborn and arrogant because they are used to being right. Meticulous people get annoyed with sloppy and careless behavior. No matter what your personality, you can find a situation that makes you uncomfortable or less effective and another personality that clashes with yours.

Besides this, life also presents difficulties based on beliefs, religion, ethnicity, culture, work—-you name it. This is not even taking into account the nasty stuff like disease, poverty, war, famine, abuse, and natural disasters. The truth is, pain, suffering and misery can arise in an infinite variety of ways. Many of these things are very difficult or even impossible to avoid. Why is this important? Because half the time we're not sure why we're upset about something. And most of the time we don't bother to think about the many valid reasons why other people are unhappy. It's easy to feel down when you read about a whole litany of misfortunes. It's easy to feel sorry when disaster strikes and innocent people get hurt. It's much more difficult to feel and to appreciate someone else's particular frustration.

Empathy is the accurate and specific recognition and sharing of another person's experience[18]. Accurate, because otherwise we just misunderstand the other person. Specific, because our experiences and hence the feelings that arise from them, are specific. There is an intellectual appreciation of someone else's situation, and there is the emotional response to that. You share the excitement, the despair, the emotions the other person is going through.

Even if someone seems to have it all, or appears to have it together, it doesn't mean she feels that way. You might think that she has every reason to be content. You might even be angry that everything you have done for the other person has gone unappreciated. But unless you can read minds, you never know. The only way to be sure is to give the other person a chance to express his or her feelings.

There is sometimes confusion about the words "sympathy," "compassion," "pity," and "empathy." Dictionary.com clarifies the differences as follows:

Sympathy, compassion, pity, empathy all denote the tendency, practice, or capacity to share in the feelings of others, especially their distress, sorrow, or unfulfilled desires. Sympathy is the broadest of these terms, signifying a general kinship with another's feelings, no matter of what kind: in sympathy with her yearning for peace and freedom; to extend sympathy to the bereaved. Compassion implies a deep sympathy for the sorrows or troubles of another coupled to a powerful urge to alleviate the pain or distress or to remove its source: to show compassion for homeless refugees. Pity usually suggests a kindly, but sometimes condescending, sorrow aroused by the suffering or ill fortune of others, often leading to a show of mercy: tears of pity for war casualties; to have pity on a thief driven by hunger. Empathy most often refers to a vicarious participation in the emotions, ideas, or opinions of others, the ability to imagine oneself in the condition or predicament of another: empathy with those striving to improve their lives; to feel empathy with Hamlet as one watches the play.

Empathy can be as simple as yawning as a resulting of seeing someone else yawn[19]. It could also be as simple as wincing while you watch someone hit his thumb with a hammer. Your response requires little effort. It is quite automatic. You don't have to condone or agree with the actions that caused the pain. It doesn't matter if you think it is careless to wield a hammer while you're distracted. You're simply reacting as if you were also hurt.

Empathy can serve our needs. In some situations, we find it convenient to go along with someone else's moods, especially if it is our boss. We laugh at her lousy jokes. We make a long face and say, "I'm so sorry," when she talks about her bad golf outing. We do it because we recognize the value of agreeing with someone else's sentiments. We want the boss to like us.

On the other hand, it is a whole different thing to make the emotional effort to feel a friend's pain for the purpose of helping him. In this case, showing empathy is like getting down on your knees to help your friend who is struggling under the burden of a heavy load. You are not standing next to him telling him to straighten up and soldier on. Showing empathy is like agreeing emotionally, "Yes! Your situation is very frustrating," without necessarily saying anything aloud. We have to imagine the pain and frustration our friend is going through and allow our hearts to sink in agreement. It is a humble act of emotional giving.

However, there are several things that prevent us from reaching out to others emotionally. Imagine you just warned someone to be careful with a hammer and she responded, "Leave me alone! I know what I'm doing!" If she hits her thumb afterward, you are much more likely to say, "I told you so," than to offer empathy. Your reminder to be cautious was rudely ignored. Instead of doing anything helpful, you want to retaliate with rudeness.

When you're not close to someone, you don't necessarily offer a lot of emotional affirmation. If a co-worker you hardly know has some good news, you offer your polite congratulations and you move on. If it's bad news, you say, "I'm sorry about the bad news," and then you move on. Appropriate social etiquette limits the amount of emotional solidarity we offer to others. We aren't supposed to break down and gush with an emotional outpour every time we hear bad news. Nor are we expected to be completely cold and distant. Our response is expected to be proportionate to the closeness of the underlying relationship and the severity of the issue. The polite way to offer help without overstepping boundaries is to say something gracious. By gracious, I mean using the right words and tone of voice to offer sincere help without sounding pushy, or even presuming that any help is needed. "I'm terribly sorry. Please let me know if there's *anything* I can do."

Some people may have a mental block against anything emotional. You may think of yourself as the "strong and silent type", and resist emotional involvement. It's not your style, you tell yourself. You might even yell at the other person like a drill sergeant. "Get up! Don't be so weak!" Dealing with the negative stereotypes against emotions is beyond the scope of this book, but a few simple points can be made. Emotions aren't necessarily a sign of weakness. It may feel unfamiliar or it may feel like losing control, but it doesn't have to. Not all emotional agreements are attempts to suck up or to ingratiate. Not all emotional displays are embarrassing or too forward or too revealing.

You might also feel you don't know how to offer emotional support. At the simplest, just being there with a sad face can be helpful. You should of course not do so while you are laughing inside about a joke you heard earlier that day. In other words, stay focused and remember that you're there to help. You're not just pretending to be sad to make someone feel better. You're genuinely sharing sadness.

Personality traits can also get in the way of empathy. I used to work with someone who took every opportunity to talk about his kids. Everyone in the office was tired of his stories. Talking to these types of people and trying to get empathy from them is pointless as they turn all conversations back to their favorite topic.

Understanding Unfamiliar Viewpoints

Not everything is as obvious, understandable, and relatable as a hammer to the thumb. There are times when the causes of pain are subconscious or hidden, and the frustration even deliberately suppressed. There are many factors that can affect our decisions, our actions, and the consequences that they bring. Sometimes we lose track of the reasons for our actions, or perhaps we were never entirely aware of the circumstances that prompted them in the first place.

What does it mean to put yourself in someone else's shoes? Ah! Shoes! Filipino politician Imelda Marcos had a few thousand pairs of these things[20]. What is it about shoes that make them such an obsession? Some people like shoes a lot, end of story, right? What more is there to it? I decided to figure it out. It took me days of on-and-off thinking before I got anywhere with it. I thought about fashion. I thought about women's clothing and how many different kinds there are. Shirt sleeves alone can have different lengths and styles.

Skirts can have different lengths and shapes and patterns and materials. The breakthrough came when I realized how complicated everything was. There are many options for each article of clothing. In order for the entire ensemble to work, items have to complement or highlight and not clash with one another. On top of that, there are fashion no-nos. For example, unless you are in a beauty pageant, you don't wear heels with a swimsuit.

The right pair of shoes can make or break an entire outfit. As a result, you have to be on a constant lookout for new shoes, and you travel with different shoes so you can dress appropriately for different occasions. When it all works, it's as if you put together an artistic creation. You feel proud and accomplished; especially if you mixed a cheap or old item with new things and made everything look elegant. You feel good looking pretty (or handsome if you're a guy). If someone pays you a compliment, you claim you just randomly grabbed whatever was in the closet. On the other hand, you feel self-conscious when you have to wear shoes that don't match the rest of your outfit, and you vow to never let that happen again. Fashions change, seasons change, you need to attend some function, or your feet hurt, and you need new shoes again. After a while, you just know you can never have too many shoes. Having more shoes in your closet is like having more colors on your palette. It gives you that much more freedom to mix and match and to be creative.

That just covers the reasons for having a decent shoe collection. Shopping for shoes is another thing. Just like photography and painting, you have to look at other people's work and try things for yourself. In fashion, it means you have to look at magazines, and go to the stores to see what is available, and make a note of the nice clothes others are wearing. Then you have to try things on to see how it looks on you. You have to spend the time to develop an eye for what looks good and fits your style. This has to happen constantly, because fashions change all the time.

One more thing about shoes: for better or for worse, I enjoy looking at well-dressed women. I also enjoy living in a country where I don't have to line up to buy shoes that only come in one style. In other words, I appreciate the end results of women's fashion and I enjoy the material wealth that makes it possible for women to buy lots of shoes. It's harder to complain when I also benefit from and enjoy the broader aspects of the situation.

To understand someone else's reasons, you have to put yourself aside; your own needs, biases, prejudices, your own way of thinking. Just because I can wear the same pair of shoes five days in a row doesn't mean that I can assume the same applies to everyone. It doesn't mean I can't think about the overall role shoes play in women's fashion. It doesn't mean I can't have a little bit of appreciation for what women go through for shoes. Just because you are a man, woman, parent, child, boss, worker, salesperson, etc., it doesn't mean you can't think about the issues facing another person.

When the reasons for other people's actions aren't obvious, you have to use your imagination and try to live in their world. It might take days to get an idea of what the other person is going through. You might have to ask questions and do some research. You have to get back to the basics. What is the context? In this case, it's women's wide variety of clothing options. What is the person trying to do within that context?

What are the goals? In this example, it is to create a pleasing ensemble. What are the rewards, costs, and challenges? The rewards include looking and feeling good, and a sense of accomplishment. The costs include money, time spent shopping, and doing terrible things to your poor feet. The challenges include sticking to your budget and not overflowing your closet. In a tragedy, what is the loss? Where is the injustice? When you are able to appreciate the constraints or challenges the other person is under, and the choices or the compromises they have to make, then you can imagine what they might be feeling, then you can wince as if the hammer hit your own thumb.

Whenever we have a disagreement or don't otherwise understand someone else, our first reaction is not usually to think about the other person's position. Usually, we just try to be more forceful with our arguments. All we need is to perceive an attack, an accusation, an insult, or any threat to our self-interest and our fight-or-flight response kicks in. The stimulus doesn't even have to be intentional or real.

Thinking about accessorizing with shoes is foreign to many men, so it may require effort on our part to understand and not judge or denigrate the amount of time and energy women devote to fashion. Making this leap of understanding to another person's experience is crucial for good listeners. It comes up in many contexts: an adult trying to understand the social, economic and psychological pressures on a teenager, or a salesperson who can't relate to a customer's loyalty to one brand over another. It takes effort for a doctor to imagine what a patient is going through during a procedure she's never undergone, herself. To break through a stalemate and reach a genuine compromise, both sides have to make the effort to understand what the other is going through.

It's easy to just say all men are pigs, all women are crazy, all teenagers are inscrutable, and all old people are stubborn. We might even use these thoughts to rationalize our own inconsiderate behaviors. But preconceived notions and stereotypes don't advance our understanding or help us to appreciate other people's positions. Our judgment is also affected if our self-interest is involved—if we stand to gain or lose something. If I had been forced to wait for my girlfriend at a shoe store, I wouldn't have been in the mood to understand shoe shopping. "Hurry up! You have too many shoes already!" If I felt my girlfriend was spending too much money on shoes she hardly wore, I wouldn't have been sympathetic. In fact, a lot of times we believe we are selfless or concerned when we actually want something for ourselves. "Come on! Let's go! You're always saying you hate heels anyway."

My neighbor has a golden retriever. I never had a dog and I still have lots of ignorant questions about pets. "Why are dogs so excited about going out for walks anyway?" I asked my neighbor.

"It smells different every day," my neighbor answered matter-of-factly.

"Ah," I said, feeling a little bit of my ignorance being dispelled.

As this example shows, it is even possible to appreciate how animals might perceive things. The important thing is not to assume there is an insurmountable gulf of comprehension and to go ahead and imagine the other's experience.

Denial is another response that can interfere with empathy. If you find yourself saying, "I can't see why he thinks that!" or, "I can't understand why she always does that!" you're not putting yourself in the other person's shoes. What you're actually saying is, "He shouldn't think that!" and, "She shouldn't do that!" If you say, "I've tried everything. Nothing works!" you have given up. All you are managing to do is to voice your dissatisfaction and frustration. This doesn't mean you shouldn't be shocked or frustrated or that your feelings aren't valid. Rather, you have to put aside your indignation for a moment and think about the other's position.

I am glad that it is easier for me as a man to meet my simple (some would say uninspired) fashion needs. After I thought about it, I realized that it takes budgeting, shopping and fashion skills to manage a woman's shoe (and fashion) collection. If I hadn't wondered about these challenges, I wouldn't have been fully able to appreciate the difficulties. Without an appreciation of the difficulties, it is much harder to have sympathy, or to actually feel the other person's frustration. Having some understanding and appreciation doesn't mean that I now have to go out and buy lots of shoes for myself. Women's fashion needs and standards don't apply to me. But I do feel I can empathize at least somewhat with the situation. As far as I can tell, their fashion demands are higher than mine, and women need to work harder to meet those demands. I still don't like to be forced to wait at the shoe store with nothing to do. But I am less likely to get upset while waiting. And I try to bring a book or we agree to meet up at a certain time. I don't feel like I am wasting my time, and my girlfriend doesn't feel rushed.

<u>Exercise—Guys Versus Gals</u>

What are the challenges of being Prince Charming, or an ideal romantic, whatever that means? What are the challenges of being assertive and protective, and being sensitive? What are the challenges of being gentle and manly, at the same time?

What are the challenges for women to have children, while pursuing a career? What are the challenges for women to stay sexy and attractive, day in and day out?

MAKE IT RELATABLE

Even if you have firsthand experience of something, it still isn't always easy to describe it and to make it relatable. With all the things people have to do, who has the time, energy and patience to explain everything to someone else? Ask women why they need to buy shoes and they might not be able to explain it succinctly. Why? Because they don't spend every day thinking about the best way to explain the subject. Now, if you were a shoe designer or worked in the marketing department of a shoe manufacturer, you would probably have some pretty interesting things to say about shoes. In other words, if it was your job to talk about shoes, you would be darn good at it. In this sense, it is the job of psychologists, psychiatrists and counselors to be able to talk about feelings and psychological processes. Writers who create compelling characters and dramatic conflicts between those characters can also be adept at working with feelings and personalities.

Television broadcasts of sports games often include former players as guest commentators. But the guest comments aren't always scintillating. The delivery isn't always smooth. The timing and phrases are sometimes awkward. It takes skill and practice to capture the essence of a game: the anticipation, the rivalry, the flow, the excitement, the hits, and the misses. When you have a good commentator, the game is much more fun. With a good commentator, you are engaged verbally and intellectually. "He fakes to the left, moves to the right, and scores!" Just turn off the sound when you watch the next game if you have any doubts. Similarly, one of the best things we can do as a listener is to help other people more accurately sound out their feelings, to provide better commentary on what is happening, to describe what they are feeling and why they are upset. Canadian literary critic Northrop Frye wrote:

> … ideas do not exist until they have been incorporated into words. Until that point you don't know whether you are pregnant or just have gas on the stomach. The operation of thinking is the practice of articulating ideas until they are in the right words.[21]

In an article in the NeuroLeadership Journal, Matthew Lieberman states:

> We have also demonstrated evidence suggesting that putting feelings into words serves as an unexpected gateway into the brain's braking system, setting self-control processes in motion without the individual intentionally trying to engage self-control.[22]

Let us also not forget that Mark Twain said:

> The difference between the right word and the almost right word is the difference between lightning and a lightning bug.

As listeners we can help speakers find better ways to express the struggles and the triumphs and the losses and the disappointments they are facing. Accurate, lively descriptions and clear, reasoned explanations are important. We can help them give expression to nebulous ideas and feelings, and perhaps in the process also help them to calm down. We can of course sigh in sympathy when someone tells us her boss rejected her recommendations. But we can do better by accurately describing what happened: "Sigh! It's really frustrating when your hard work and good ideas aren't appreciated!"

A lot of things in life are nuanced and complicated. There are a lot of variables and moving parts. Many of life's dilemmas and choices are not easily summed up in a few words. Many traditions and practices cannot easily be described in a few sentences. We manage it reasonably well because we learn or adapt bit by bit until it becomes routine and just another part of our lives. But ask us to explain the intricacies, the highs and lows, of an activity, and we might be caught tongue-tied. When things go wrong with these activities, it can be hard to explain our feelings and reasons to someone else. It's hard to explain why you need to spend more time shopping when someone else is becoming impatient with you. It's hard to explain why the game is important when someone is nagging you. In a crisis, or when we are distraught, it gets even more difficult. In an argument, you are long past the point of rationally appreciating each other's viewpoints. You just want to win.

When I try to recall the things that have affected my view toward compassion, a few influences come to mind. Books like Victor Hugo's *Les Miserables* and the Shakespearean tragedies remind me of how bad things can be. Ordinary news stories are too brief to give more than a glimpse into the lives of those hit with misfortune. With a novel, you can get to know the characters more intimately. You can watch as some characters make sacrifices as they grapple with right and wrong. You can watch as other characters scheme and plot for personal gain. With a work of fiction, you are supposed to feel for the characters. The author has done all the work to make that as easy as possible.

Another influence, and one I will never forget, was my experience volunteering at a telephone crisis center. I remember having deep conversations with people and admiring their courage in the face of adversity. I remember being manipulated by callers. I remember callers with dark events in their past expressing clear hope for the future. Together, these experiences have allowed me to think more concretely about good and evil, adversity and triumph. The more you imagine yourself in other people's positions, seeing from their perspectives, appreciating their excitement and disappointment, the risks and rewards they face, the easier it is to find compassion for others.

To sum it up, life is hard for everyone, for many different reasons. Our hopes and dreams, as Obama said after the Tucson shootings, and also our destinies are bound together. It can be easy to show empathy in simple situations. In other situations, we may not know how to reach out emotionally, or we feel it is awkward or inappropriate. In addition, other people's pain and suffering is not always obvious, easily understood, or easily accessed and relatable. Understanding an unfamiliar point of view can be hard for several reasons. First, we might have to get over our own frustration. Second, we have to be open to the possibility that other people may have understandable reasons for their behavior. Third, it requires thinking and imagining ourselves in someone else's position. This can take time and research. You have to look at the other person's basic values, the constraints or challenges they are under, and the choices or the compromises they have to make. You have to try to appreciate the loss and injustice they face.

Exercise—Empathy Starts At Home

What negative stereotypes or generalizations do you use to describe others? For example, "They're all lazy!" Or, "They don't care." Do these generalizations help you appreciate others' unique situations?

Continuing along the same lines as the previous exercise, what are some of the difficulties or challenges facing your family members? Be as specific as possible, based on gender, role, personality, etc. What are the constraints they are under? What are the choices and compromises they have to make?

What are some of the difficulties or challenges facing teenagers in general?

What are some of the difficulties or challenges of being feminine or masculine?

What are some of your fears and frustrations?

What is the saddest piece of fictional work you have read, or the saddest piece of music you have heard? How did it affect you?

Exercise—"I Hate the People at Work!"

While you may have valid reasons for not liking the people you work with, you can still think about the broader issues affecting different people in your business circle.

What are some of the difficulties or challenges facing your co-workers? Be as specific as possible.

What are some of the difficulties or challenges facing your customers?

What are some of the difficulties or challenges facing business owners or workers in general?

What are some of the difficulties or challenges in your industry or line of work?

Exercise—"Imagine"[*]

One of the more common ways we come in contact with other countries is through imported food and manufactured goods. What is your favorite

---

[*]   1971 song "Imagine" by John Lennon

international food? Where do the beans used to make your coffee or chocolate come from?

How many different countries do the objects around your house come from? You can have a competition with other family members to see who comes up with the most countries.

Next, you can look at the broader issues facing people around the world:

What are some of the artistic, scientific, economic, and cultural achievements of other countries? And what challenges do they face?

Since appreciating different people's unique situations can be a huge task, you are encouraged to visit my website www.8StepListen.com. Look under the topic "Understanding others" in the Forum section. You can share your views and vote on posts that help you understand where other people are coming from.

———

Summary

Empathy requires effort. It can be simple or complicated. You need to get over your own frustrations with the situation. You have to be prepared to accept that maybe other people have understandable reasons for their actions. It requires you to step aside and to think about the constraints, the choices, and the compromises that face the other person.

Knowing how empathy works gives you the tremendous ability to promote understanding and to resolve differences. This in turn allows you to reach people and build meaningful relationships.

Now that we have looked at empathy, let us take a closer look at how we talk.

Chapter 4 Not All Talk Is Equal

"The biggest mistake is believing there is one right way to listen, to talk, to have a conversation—or a relationship."
Deborah Tannen

T he first problem with listening is that the word itself describes too many things. It is used loosely to describe one half of a whole range of communications between two people. Two people can share a juicy piece of gossip. One person can give instructions to another. Or someone can console a friend after a family loss. When you consider the rich and varied conversations that can take place between two people, it is obvious that the listening half of any such exchange must also be similarly rich and varied—and indeed it is.

Therefore, to understand listening we need first to take a step back and take a closer look at conversations in general. There is more than one way that people can interact with one another. What type of interaction we have determines the kind of conversation we have. This in turn influences not just how we speak, but also how we listen. In some conversations, the listening is almost a secondary goal, or just an initial requirement. In some conversations, it is a key component. If you went to a cafe and observed the people sitting around you, you might see people engaged in a friendly chat about the weather, or two friends sharing stories about their weekend activities. There could be a lively debate about political issues at another table, or maybe even an argument over a heated topic at a fourth table. We are all familiar with these kinds of conversations. But there are other ways we can interact with others.

ADVISING

One day I was waiting for a ferry when some tourists approached me for directions.

"Does this ferry go downtown?" asked the man who must have been the father. He spoke with a foreign accent.

"Yes, it does," I answered.

"Does this go to the big museum?" he continued.

"No, the museum is on this side of the harbor," I said.

"Ah, yes. Of course," the father answered. He seemed to remember seeing something from a tourist map.

"We want to go to the financial district," he said, returning to his original goal.

"Right, stay here and wait for the next ferry."

When you are giving directions or being an advisor in general, you start off your listening with some pretty clear goals. You want to narrow down and get to the specifics. Where is the other person trying to go? What are they trying to do? What is the problem? Where do they need help? If the speaker seems to be going in two different directions at once, you let him know. "No, the museum is on this side of the harbor." Once you know what the other person is looking for, you give instructions and you send him off. Being an advisor is quick, and arguably efficient. But giving instructions and advice has its drawbacks too. Doing so does not foster initiative. It doesn't encourage thinking and exploring. Furthermore, there are many decisions that cannot easily be decided based on someone else's advice and instructions. For example, should you change careers to pursue a life-long passion? Should you start or end a relationship? How should you raise your children?

Sometimes we deliberately want to dismiss people with gratuitous advice. You may have heard a complaint for the tenth time.

"I swear I'm going to give him a piece of my mind!"

"Yes, you should! Either that or quit! Just please stop complaining!"

You may simply not wish to deal with unpleasant stories, or perhaps someone is giving you too much information, or you are too busy to deal with something.

"You know, I've been having problems in bed…"

"Right! Try taking a sleeping pill. So what do you think about tomorrow's game?"

"Mommy! Mommy! Scott's not playing fair!"

"Then don't play with Scott! Watch some TV!"

As you can see in these examples, giving advice can seem like you don't care or that you're annoyed. If you do find yourself frequently telling people what to do, just make sure your advice is appropriate and that you're not discouraging people from approaching you with a serious issue.

SERVING THE SPEAKER

There are other ways to assist someone besides giving advice and instructions. It's possible for someone to serve another person's need to express something or to talk things out by being a sounding board. You can consciously help the other person to explore ideas and to question assumptions. It is also possible to help the other person by providing emotional support and encouragement.

For example, a mother could be listening to a small child's random chatter. Or someone could be listening to a friend talk about a recent overseas trip. You serve the other person primarily by listening to them, by being an "Audience." A lot of times the listener simply has to say a few simple things to prod the speaker to keep going. "Ah, huh." "Then what happened?" "That sounds fun!" I discuss this kind of listening in much more detail in Chapter 5.

Perhaps your wife has a lot of ideas about how to redecorate the living room. She wants to bounce ideas off you, and also solicit your input on colors and patterns. In this case, you need to do more than simply nod your head and go, "Uh huh." You wife doesn't just want to tell you what she wants to do. She wants you to contribute in a meaningful way as well. You may have to say, "Uh huh... Maybe some lighter colors would brighten things up in this room." In this kind of listening, you have to be a little more involved, not to the point where you take over or make the other person give up. After all, you may not want to own the redecoration project. You certainly don't want to take away any of your wife's excitement or enthusiasm. Your wife may just want some input from you so she feels you have participated. You just have to be involved enough to help out in a non-intrusive manner. I call this being a "Contributor." I talk about this in more detail in Chapter 6.

However, things get more interesting if the emotional stakes are higher. If your friend just lost his job and is falling behind on his mortgage payments, how would you listen to him? How would you listen to a family member who has just been through a tragedy? How would you listen to a friend struggling through a marriage that is on the rocks? You cannot simply nod and say, "Uh huh." You cannot simply suggest she get over it and move on. That could be perceived as a very insensitive remark. Until the other person has grieved or fully digested the relevant emotion, he is not ready to move on. Instead, you have to listen and be patient, understanding, compassionate, and organized. You have to listen as if you were a "Counselor." Chapter 7 discusses how you might accomplish this.

Here again is a summary of the ways we can serve someone else by listening, together with some examples.

Audience
Listen to a child's random chatter
Listen to someone talk about her day or tell a story
Listen to a juicy piece of gossip
Listen to someone talk about one of his passions

Contributor
Listen to someone talk through the planning or coordination of some activity (planning a wedding, planning a marketing campaign, etc.)
Listen to someone work out an idea or express a feeling for the first time
Listen to a frustrated customer

Counselor
Listen to someone describing going through a significant event
Listen to someone in a crisis
Listen to someone express doubts about achieving a goal

I was once talking about my idea that a listener can serve a speaker. My friend Chris immediately said the word "serve" has a lot of meanings. "Do you mean like a waiter?" she asked. I said yes, just like a waiter, sometimes you have to be attentive without being obtrusive. Good waiters fill your glass before you notice it's empty. Good waiters don't interrupt you while you are chewing or having an intimate discussion. Good waiters don't interfere, and can certainly enhance your dining experience. Similarly, good listeners can let you get into the experience of talking things out without you necessarily knowing how they did it. Under different circumstances, good listeners can serve as adept party hosts. Hosts organize food and entertainment and make it possible for the guests to have fun. But they don't tell their guests how to do it. They don't constantly remind their guests to use a coaster or not to touch the stereo. As a listener, you can sometimes facilitate the conditions for someone to talk things out. Just as you can be a gracious party host, you can also be a gracious listener. You can be accommodating and flexible without being overbearing or controlling. Good listeners can also serve as wise friends. They're not there to give advice or quick answers. They help the person discover their own solutions. They are here to serve the other person's need to talk through fears and frustrations and sound out ideas on how to make changes.

This list of listener roles is not meant to be exhaustive. These are not absolute categories either. Conversations can drift from one type to another. Roles can switch back and forth. It is not necessarily productive to think about listening styles or methods as absolutely right or definitely wrong. However, if you only know one method, you will most likely encounter difficulties if you try to use it in every situation. Flexibility and using the appropriate tools will often provide better results. Some situations call for swift and direct instructions, while others are more suited to guided discovery.

Problems can obviously occur if the two sides are not engaged in the same kind of conversation. You are not playing the same game. You may be trying to tell a story but your husband thinks you are looking for advice and starts giving you all kinds of suggestions. You may want to cry about something, but your friend starts telling you how sad she was the day her pet died. Sure, you listened to the story and tried to be helpful by giving suggestions, but you failed to realize that was not what your wife was looking for. Yes, you heard how sad your friend was, but you jumped in too soon with your own story.

Other habits can cause problems too. Perhaps you grew up in a large, boisterous family and the only way to be heard at the dinner table was to just interrupt. Perhaps you were rewarded at school for speaking up before the other kids. These mismatches and poor habits inevitably lead to dissatisfaction in one or both parties. This is different from not paying attention. If you are not paying attention, then you are not even playing at all.

If you listen for the purpose of having an everyday conversation or debate, then you will constantly be thinking about how to respond and what to say next. If you listen for the purpose of fixing something and providing a solution, then you will not give the other person a chance to talk through his own ideas. But as we have just discussed, you can concentrate on the other person's speaking needs. You are giving the other person every opportunity to voice and work through her ideas and feelings. You don't, in the usual sense, have any point to make. You help with the momentum and continuity of their stories by appropriate questioning and prompting: "And then what happened?" You convey your understanding by paraphrasing. You summarize and generalize the ideas. You help them find words to describe their anxiety and frustration, without putting words into their mouths. You help them find their own answers, without telling them what to do or how to do it.

Recognize that people talk for different reasons and adjust your listening accordingly for the best results. Be a little more attentive and unobtrusive with your listening and you'll find more customers. Be more gracious and accommodating with your listening and you'll find yourself more popular. Be wise and patient with your listening and you'll find people opening up to you and showing you more respect. When was the last time you served someone else as a listener? When was the last time you consciously made it about the other person and listened, whether it was a customer, your spouse, your kids, or your subordinates? The single most important thing you can do is to recognize that you don't always have to give advice or trade stories or even say much. There are a variety of tools out there. People have different speaking needs. Satisfy those speaking needs. Mix it up a little.

EXAMPLE

A couple and their infant are at a family gathering. The husband's mother plays with the child. The wife overhears her mother-in-law say, "You're so cute! It's such a shame your mother can't dress you nicely." On the drive home, the wife is fuming. The husband asks his wife what happened. She repeats her mother-in-law's comment. Should the husband:

a) tell his wife to calm down, or to stop over-reacting over an off-hand remark.

b) agree with his mother. The outfit was pretty goofy.

c) respond with another story of how his mother insulted someone else.

d) implore his wife not to fight with his mother.

e) suggest to his wife that she should go buy some new baby clothes.

Let's say the husband tells his wife to calm down.

"No!" she replies. "Your mother was out of line! We were late and I didn't have time to dress him."

"It's no big deal," says the husband, not wanting to take sides or get into any trouble.

Now the wife is even more upset. They don't talk the rest of the way home.

The next day, the wife tells the husband that they're going to the mall to shop for baby clothes. The husband mumbles something about the cost of baby clothes and something about wanting to watch a game. They get into another fight.

The first problem with the multiple choice options above is that none of them serve the wife's need to express her frustration. What you're thinking, your state of mind as you enter a conversation makes a huge difference. If you're impatient, annoyed, defensive, or just tired, your responses will reflect that.

"What's the problem now?"

"Not again!"

"I don't want to deal with this."

With these kinds of thoughts going through your head, you'll find yourself cutting off the other person and defending your position. It isn't always appropriate to think about having a shared conversation or to concentrate on problem-solving either. Instead, remind yourself to just let the other person talk. Serve their speaking needs and you'll fair much better.

Second, the options above don't convey empathy for what the wife is feeling. When you make a comment about a woman's parenting skills, she might become really offended. She might feel being a good mother is part of her identity. It's part of who she is as a person. Calling a man "weak" is similar to that. Wives also want to know that their husbands will support them if there's a disagreement with the mother-in-law. It's the same as wanting your wife to take your side if you have a disagreement with your boss. If your wife doesn't support you, you feel you're all alone battling everyone.

What if the husband thinks about his mother's comment and how it might have made his wife feel? He might suddenly remember how he felt when his father-in-law insulted him.

"I thought about what my mom said. I remembered when your dad called me 'just a plumber'."

"Go on," says the wife.

"I'm sorry. My mother shouldn't have said that. It was inappropriate."

"Yes it was," the wife agrees.

"I also didn't back you up," continues the husband.

"No you didn't."

"I appreciate all the things you do around the house. You're a great mother."

Listening isn't necessary about solving problems. You can't control what in-laws say or do, nor are you usually expected to. But you can certainly listen and support each other. Remember to serve other people's need to express themselves, and remember to empathize with their feelings.

SUMMARY

Sometimes you need to listen to someone simply as an audience. You already know from daily life how to do this. You may not do it as often as you should or as well as you could. Chapter 5 will give you more information on being an audience. Sometimes you need to make meaningful contributions to a conversation. You should do this only if you have something of value to contribute. You should assist without depriving the other person of any sense of accomplishment or sense of ownership. Chapter 6 provides more details on how to be a good contributor. And then on those unfortunate occasions when life deals us a bad hand, you may have to be there as a counselor for someone else. That is covered in Chapter 7.

Chapter 5 The Audience Is King

You have to respect your audience. Without them, you're essentially standing alone, singing to yourself.
KD Lang

My play was a complete success. The audience was a failure.
Ashleigh Brilliant

E very once in a while something uncommon or unusual happens. When it does, we want to share the news with someone.

"You won't believe what I saw today!"
"Check out my new cell phone!"
"Mommy! Mommy!"
"Guess what my broker told me today."

On other occasions, our aggravation or anxiety is provoked.

"My job sucks!"
"I hope this economy improves soon."
"People should learn how to drive!"
"It is so hard to return products to your company!"

When this happens, we want someone to hear our complaints. Whether we have something to say or something to complain about, we want someone to listen to us and identify with the underlying sentiment. When you listen to someone share or tell a story, you're an audience of one.

To understand how to really listen as an audience, let's look at how we listen to music. I like to listen to the radio when I'm driving. A lot of people like to listen to music when they're exercising. Most of us like to have a little music in the background as we go about our daily business, but we're not really engaged, listening to it fully. However, if I go to a live concert, I might sway side to side during a love song. I might jump up and down during a more upbeat piece. I am emotionally involved in the performance! In addition, I clap and whistle loudly at the end of the show to demonstrate my appreciation.

A concert is not a concert without an audience. Knowing that an audience will respond to the songs and cheer at the end of the performance makes a huge difference. Imagine a fictitious society where people attend artistic performances but never react during the show and never clap or make a sound at the end. The artists would have no way of knowing if their performance is moving the audience. At the end of the show, the audience just got up and left. How strange it would be! A great deal of feedback and satisfaction would be taken away from *both* the performers and the audience if that were to happen. Alternatively, imagine a comedy where the audience comes out teary-eyed, or a tragedy where the audience is laughing throughout. How odd is that?

What do you need to do to be a good audience of one? Being a good audience has three parts. First, you have to recognize that someone thinks she has something interesting to say or something to get off her chest. The show has started. You should not treat her as background noise or music. Second, give the other person a chance to speak and engage emotionally with her if it is appropriate. Listen attentively, sway or dance if it moves you. Third, acknowledge the story. Clap or whistle at the end.

Audience Steps
1) Recognize someone has something to say.
2) Let her speak. Engage emotionally if appropriate.
3) Acknowledge the story.

You Got Something To Say?

Often you can tell someone has something he wants to share because there's an exclamation that is supposed to raise the listener's attention. Or he makes a general complaint that invites the listener to ask for more details. Or he makes an outrageous statement. The following list shows examples of these, together with responses that encourage the speaker to continue.

Raising listener's attention or inviting query

Exclamation: "You won't believe what I saw today!"
Response: "What did you see today?"

Exclamation: "Mommy! Mommy!"
Response: "Yes, dear?"

Complaint: "My job sucks!"
Response: "Did your manager or co-workers or customers do something aggravating again?"

Complaint: "People should learn how to drive!"
Response: "Did someone cut you off?"

Complaint: "It is so hard to return products to your company!"
Response: "Can you tell me what difficulties you encountered, sir?"

Exaggeration: "I'm quitting school!"
Response: "Let's talk about your concerns with school."

Anxious: "I hope this economy improves soon."
Response: "Did you have bad news at the office?"

Listening as an audience is simple in some situations. Most of us know how to respond when someone says, "Check out my new cell phone!" We ask for a demonstration and we ask about the cool new features. We recognize the speaker has something to share and we know how to engage and draw out her excitement. We don't say the following:

"It's okay, but that model's not that cool." This completely dampens the speaker's excitement.

"Just wait until the next model comes out and you won't be this excited anymore." This also rains on the speaker's parade, as if his excitement was something to be fixed.

"Why did you buy that?" This is questioning the soundness of the purchase.

"I got a new cell phone too! Look at mine!" This redirects attention from the speaker to the listener.

"But the new version is coming out next month." This is second-guessing the speaker's actions.

"Your cell phone is so much better than mine!" This is a more passive way to redirect attention from the speaker to the listener.

In this context, it is easy to see that these responses are inappropriate. But when someone wants to share something that isn't fun or exciting, or we don't see why we should simply let the other person tell their story, we often make these mistakes. We don't share the other person's feelings and concerns. We don't ask for more information and draw him out. For example, he says, "I'm worried about my project." We respond:

"It can't be that bad, you're almost done." This minimizes the problem and dampens the speaker's desire to continue.

"Why don't you talk to your boss? I'm sure you can work something out." This presumes there is an easy fix, and once again discourages the speaker from sharing his anxiety and continuing with his story.

"Why? Did you mess up?" This is questioning the speaker's ability. It puts the speaker on defense. Now he has to prove his innocence first.

"I know! I'm worried about my project too." This distracts the speaker by shifting the focus onto us.

"But the customer just gave you some good feedback." This is second-guessing the speaker's concerns about his project.

"Your project is so much better than mine!" Again, this is a more passive way to redirect attention from the speaker to the listener.

While men may like to offer fixes, and women may like to share stories in order to bond, all these responses make it harder for the speaker to proceed with his story. Of course I'd rather see the latest must-have gadget than talk about problems, especially if I'm part of the problem. I deliberately used our interest in cell phones to illustrate two things. One, we are excellent audiences under the right circumstances and with the proper motivation. Two, we don't use these excellent skills as often as we can and we make a number of mistakes instead.

Next time, when you notice yourself about to use one of the responses above, take a second to think about what is happening. The other person might simply be trying to share an emotion. He might just be venting. Take the cue and settle down to listen as an audience.

Draw Them Out, Engage Them

After the speaker starts her story, make sure you allow her to tell it. Use the listening skills described in Chapter 2 and 3 to draw her out and engage her. If you ask a question that's a little too penetrating, you might hear the other person say, "Wait! I'll get to that in a minute." In other words, the speaker is telling you to sit back, not interrupt, and just let the story unfold. Try not to one-up or top the story. "I've seen better features on other cell phones." It isn't a challenge. Avoid making suggestions on how the acting could have been better or claim that you were there too and that's not how you remember it. "You're wrong, this cell phone has two cameras." It's not a story-telling competition. Try not to give suggestions or advice on what the characters in the story could have or should have done. "You should talk about the games and applications on this phone. That's what makes it special." The speaker isn't looking for advice on how to tell stories. It will take all the wind out of her sail. Avoid heckling, too. In other words, act like it's a good concert, movie or television show you are watching and be a polite, appreciative audience.

In the middle of the conversation, you may have to prompt the speaker: "Can the cell phone record movies too?" If it's a story, you can cheer her on: "What happened next? And then what did you do?" You can says things like, "Uh huh", "Keep going", "I'm with you", "Go ahead", to encourage the speaker to continue. You can nod your head and use gestures to encourage the speaker.

APPLAUD

What do you do towards the end of the conversation? Here is a sample dialogue between a mother and a child:

"Mommy! Mommy!"

"Yes, dear?"

"I drew something!"

"What is it? It's an apple! That's a nice, red apple!"

"This is my apple!"

"What else can you draw?"

The point isn't whether the drawing was good. The child wasn't looking for advice on how to draw. If mommy hadn't looked, the child most likely would have continued to seek mommy's attention by tugging at her dress. If mommy hadn't recognized and praised the apple, the child wouldn't have been satisfied either. Sincere affirmation is as important as applause at the end of a performance. This isn't to say that we should treat each other like children. Our need to share doesn't diminish with age. Just look at all the social networking sites and videos that go viral on the Internet. When we come across something novel and amusing, or something that touches us, we want to share our amusement or feelings.

Consider this slightly more grown-up exchange:

Neilson: "I lined up for hours to buy this tablet computer!"

Cecilia: "Wow! Can I see it?"

Neilson: "Of course! Let me turn it on."

Cecilia: "This thing is so cool! I need to start saving money!"

If Cecilia hadn't made that jealous remark about saving money, or something else that recognized Neilson's effort and satisfaction, Neilson wouldn't have been happy. In other words, at the end of the story, remember to laugh or weep or cheer or applaud to demonstrate your genuine appreciation. Acknowledge the sentiment. Refrain from over-reacting, however. If you scream and shout and give a standing ovation after an obviously mediocre effort, people will just think you're strange.

Exercise—"Can You Hear Me Now?"†

Try to identify situations where you could be a better audience. For example, you can listen to your family members talk about their hobbies or their day. "How was your day?" "How did soccer practice go? Did you learn any new moves?"

Give subordinates a chance to talk about the ups and downs of their work. Try to do it without micromanaging.

Give customers a chance to talk about their experiences in using your product and services, or about the challenges they face.

EVERYDAY SITUATIONS

There is a special case of being an audience of one. You can make it exciting for someone to talk about one of his passions. You can make it possible for someone to go on and on about his thoughts. Once, during a holiday visit, I found myself sitting in the back seat of a mini-van with a couple of four-year-olds. Perhaps in an

† Catchphrase for Verizon Wireless commercial touting their network's coverage.

attempt to entertain them, I started doing cartoon voices. This then prompted one of the kids to re-tell the entire episode of her favorite cartoon. Her sentences were a bit jumbled because of her young age, but she was excited and she kept talking. "And then…" she said. "Oh dear, what happened next?" I asked, to help her keep up the momentum.

Normally we try to be polite and hold back on talking at length about our passions. The reason is we usually don't expect others to be as interested in our hobbies and pet peeves as we are. We don't wish to bore others with details. But if someone shows genuine interest and curiosity, we are often delighted to launch into a big discussion of our favorite topic. If you can recall terms and concepts that have always confused you, you can bring them up and ask for the expert to clarify and give you a more in-depth explanation. All those questions you were too afraid to ask? Well, go ahead and ask! I once ran into someone who collected tennis racquets. So I asked him about sweet spots and how racquet technology has changed over the years. He went on and on for an hour!

When you use terms particular to a subject, you signal to the other person that he can delve into more detail. When you add to the discussion instead of moving on to the next subject, you encourage the other person to continue. If someone is excited about a new laptop computer that will be introduced into the market, you can say, "Yes, I heard the laptop is really thin and light!"

Keep in mind, though, there is a big difference between asking someone to give you a crash course, versus allowing him to convey his excitement on the subject. I remember a colleague asking me to explain computer databases to him in five minutes because he needed to ask some intelligent questions about it in a meeting that was coming up in fifteen minutes. I felt that not only was he not interested in the subject, but he didn't value my time either.

In addition to getting someone to talk about his passions, you can also get someone to share fascinating insider stories. Or you can trade stories with people. I once listened in shock as a hotel manager told me matter-of-factly how thieves would walk off with all kinds of hotel property. Every now and again, I also trade horrifying or amusing stories with my clients and friends.

Exercise—Hobbies for $800

Try to pick an unusual topic. See if you can come up with some good questions about this topic. For example, if you're on a new date or with a new client and she mentions kites or bonsai, what questions would you ask to get her to elaborate on the subject? (Yes, I deliberately choose situations where you stand to gain something by building rapport.)

————

As a listener, we should also be aware that people exaggerate. Sometimes we exaggerate for comedic effect. All the "Your mother is so fat…" jokes are based on exaggeration. Sometimes we exaggerate to highlight our frustration. "I'm going to quit this stupid job and go join a circus!" "I'm going to hit the next person who says 'paradigm' or 'think outside the box'!" We're not necessarily going to join the circus or hit anyone. We just feel so frustrated that we want to do those things. If we're allowed to talk about the reasons for our frustrations, we'll most likely calm down and forget about the exaggerated statements.

Sometimes we also deliberately say things to annoy someone or to pick a fight. Or we might do the opposite and give someone the silent treatment. A few years ago I took ballroom dancing lessons. The teachers were a husband-and-wife team. One day, the wife was noticeably upset and ignored the husband the entire lesson. Imagine the two teachers showing the students all the different dance moves. The husband kept explaining the moves as the wife danced with him while wearing a barely concealed scowl on her face! The husband even said, "In dancing, the man always leads, just as he should in real life," in an attempt to get some kind of reaction from his wife. She just kept ignoring him.

Once in a while, you have to do a bit more to get someone to talk. This could be a patient who is embarrassed about something. Or it could be a spouse, subordinate or a child who is afraid to bring something up. In this case you have to be observant and look for signs that the speaker is acting different or on edge. Then put the person at ease and encourage him to speak his mind.

Listening skills can also be used to great comedic effect. If you feel a conversation is getting too serious, you can inject humor to lighten up the atmosphere. For example, my friends and I found ourselves talking about the Plaza Hotel in New York City. Ed, our resident history buff, said, "Yeah, that's where they signed the Plaza Accord."

We all stared at him.

"Yeah, they had a meeting to fix the exchange rate," Ed continued.

"I have no idea what you're talking about," I said. "But I'll tell you what I know: 'Crocodile' Dundee[‡] stayed at the Plaza Hotel!"

If you hear something odd or out of place, you can jump on it and take it to its absurd, funny conclusion. We were having lunch one day when my friend Katherine mentioned that she wanted to lose ten pounds before her young nephew's birthday celebration. "Why?" I asked earnestly, "Are you going to wear a bikini and jump out of his cake?" She was surprised for a second and then she laughed. Just remember, have fun, but try not to be mean while you're doing it.

RELATIONSHIP LISTENING

In the dating process, there are many, many opportunities to be an audience for each other. There comes a time when you have to warn each other about your bad habits. "By the way, there's something you should know about me…" There comes a time when you have to warn each other about your crazy family problems. "By the way, there's something you should know about my parents…" Being a good audience in this case means handling the embarrassment, the "I don't want to scare you" factor, acknowledging the

---

[‡]   Main character from the 1986 Australian movie "'Crocodile' Dundee", where several scenes took place at the Plaza Hotel in New York City.

uniqueness of the described situation, and empathizing with the person.

As couples get to know each other better, they start sharing their past. "I've never told anyone this. When I was a kid..." This is an example of an opening to a childhood story. Maybe the story involves a toy that was longed for but never received. Maybe it involves fighting parents. Maybe it's a story involving a loss of innocence. The stories from our past may seem a little childish or foolish in the eyes of another adult. These stories have to be heard almost as if you're still talking to the child from years ago.

Sharing hopes and aspirations is another thing that couples do. Here we have to respect the stated wishes and be sensitive to any underlying needs behind these hopes and aspirations. A desire to change careers may be fueled by a childhood passion, a desire to make a difference, a wish to get away from an unfulfilling job, a need for security, or some other combination of reasons.

While married couples don't always pay attention to each other as if they're playing a high-stakes poker game, they often share a general awareness of each other. Imagine a couple at the breakfast table. They're both absorbed in their respective newspaper sections.

"Can you pass me the bread, please?"

The husband pushes the bread over to the other side of the table.

"Thanks, honey."

"You're welcome."

They both continue reading their newspapers. On the whole, however, couples need to be good audiences for each other's entire lives, not only in the listening sense. You show concern and ask questions about each other's days. You do little things for each other to acknowledge the ups and downs of everyday life. If you notice your spouse had a rough day, you might rub her shoulders. If he had a rough week, you might suggest going out for dinner. You share your lives with each other partly by noticing what's happening and reaffirming the resulting feelings.

SUMMARY

A good audience is the basis of good listening. It is the polite way to behave when someone has something to say. The big secret here is that we can be excellent audiences under the right circumstances. We recognize people have something to share, we engage with the speaker and share his or her feelings, we acknowledge the story. We just have to be more mindful of those good listening skills and make the effort to apply them in more places.

Here are a few tips for being an audience:
1. If necessary, listener and speaker state and agree on expectations at the beginning; or, as a listener, you recognize that the speaker has something to say.
2. Pay attention to the speaker.
3. Encourage the speaker to continue. Nod, say, "Uh huh," "Keep going," etc.
4. Engage with the speaker and help him or her stay in the moment.
5. Paraphrase, summarize and generalize.
6. Try not to interrupt, one-up, make suggestions, etc.

7. Don't compete for air time; yield whenever possible.
8. Echo sentiment and acknowledge the ending of the story appropriately.

Being an audience allows you to participate for a brief moment in someone else's life. Do this well and people will find you interesting and fun to talk to.

Chapter 6 Your Contributions Are Important

The service was attentive without being obtrusive.
Common phrase describing good restaurant service.

"I have a big presentation tomorrow. Could I do a dry run with you?"
"Honey, I've been looking at lots of carpets and patterns. What do you think of these?"

The next conversational role builds on being an audience of one. You have to pay attention and be in the moment with the speaker. You have to be a good audience. But there are additional duties and differences as a contributor.

Ways to contribute to a conversation
• Ask good questions
• Help the speaker get back on track
• Help the speaker uncover a logical error or a missing step
• Help the speaker express an idea or feeling for the first time

- Make a suggestion or contribute a new idea
- Provide constructive feedback and give specific praise

The first few items on the list are a little more passive. The last few involve more input. As is often the case, there are better and worse ways to get your ideas, suggestions, and feedback across to another person. The point is, you're still serving the other person's needs. You're not trying to take over or to put your own stamp on the conversation.

THE SOUNDING BOARD

Many business and personal activities require planning and coordination. Parties, weddings, all the way up to multi-million-dollar marketing campaigns are made up of multiple, coordinated activities that have to be carried out in specific sequences. Most stories have characters and some kind of plot. Boy meets girl; relationship encounters difficulties; relationship grows or falls apart. Many conflicts involve two or more people and have some background and history. Some conflicts involve entire countries and go back hundreds of years!

It's often helpful to hear our own thoughts out loud. Sometimes, when we are deep in the middle of something, we get bogged down by details or get distracted by unrelated activities. We lose sight of the overall plan or picture. By talking things out with another person, we can sometimes jog our memories and recall things we have temporarily put aside. Or it might help us realize that we have made a mistake or missed a step. When you act as a sounding board, you're not necessarily contributing any content. You don't even necessarily have to understand what you're hearing. Sometimes you only get a glimpse of the whole. The speaker just needed a small step filled in, is happy you helped them fill it, and can gladly move on. Other times, you need to assist with the entire story from beginning to end. Being a sounding board is similar to being an audience, but you don't have to acknowledge the story or the sentiment.

A few years ago, I was asked to work on a project that was started by others and then abruptly put on hold because of unforeseen circumstances. Months later, to avoid losing the budget money, it was suddenly resurrected and put on a strict deadline. I decided to talk to my manager before I met with the client. First, I wanted to talk things out with someone within my company. I wanted to go through the complicated steps aloud to make sure I didn't miss anything or make any mistakes. Second, I wanted my manager to know how I was planning to execute the project. I wanted to keep her in the loop. I wanted to cover my ass if any glitch came up.

We talked about the project from start to finish. My manager just listened and allowed me to talk through my plan. When I got to the more complicated parts of the project, I slowed down and went into more detail. By the end of the conversation, both my manager and I felt I had things under control. A few months later, the project was concluded to the customer's satisfaction. If my proposed plan had a mistake or was missing a step, simply talking it out could have helped me uncover the problem. "Ah, yes, I should take care of this first."

"That reminds me, let me make a note so I don't forget."

Besides helping with the organization of activities, a contributor can also help the speaker express an idea or feeling. The simplest way to do this is to help someone finish their sentence. One day, I found myself talking to my English teacher about Ennio Morricone's soundtrack for the 1987 movie *The Untouchables*.

"The track for the bad guy Al Capone is so…" I hesitated.

"… full of the good, the bad, and the ugly?"

"Yeah!" I said. "How did you know?"

My teacher just rolled his eyes.

Helping someone express him or herself can also be more complicated. To use a theatrical analogy, it would be similar to helping a writer find the right words to an unfinished scene. The writer knows he has something to get off his chest. The need to explain the story to the listener forces the writer to make sense, to complete his sentences, to explain the background, the characters, the conflict and any hidden or implied assumptions.

"I have a strange feeling about this, but I can't put a finger on it."

"Okay, let's try to figure it out. What seems odd or different to you?"

We can also help people find ways to express both the mundane and the interesting things in their lives. We can help make the dull more bearable, and the exciting more memorable.

"I think it's amazing how you manage to get the kids to school every day!"

"Sounds like you really had an eye-opening trip!"

"It's a calculated risk, but it seems like you've thought it through."

Finally, one of the best ways to describe something is to compare it to something else that is more familiar. There was one weekend when I found myself at the jewelry section of a museum with my girlfriend. Since I was bored, I started asking all kinds of questions about the exhibit. "Why is the exhibit based on jewelry from one company only? Isn't that free advertising for them? What's so special about this stuff anyway?" A lady overheard me and started telling me how women liked this company's innovative and beautiful designs.

"You mean it's like shoes," I said.

"Exactly," she replied, and we all had a good laugh.

CONSTRUCTIVE FEEDBACK AND SPECIFIC PRAISE

In the book *The Last Lecture*, Randy Pausch talked about working for professor Andries "Andy" van Dam as a teaching assistant. He told the story of how he got some much-needed feedback from van Dam:

Randy, it's such a shame that people perceive you as being so arrogant, because it's going to limit what you're going to be able to accomplish in life.[23]

As a professor, van Dam had no need to be diplomatic and tactful with a lowly teaching assistant. He could have just told Pausch that "your arrogance is going to limit what you accomplish in life." He could have said, "You need to work on your people skills." But that would have been passing judgment. Instead, professor van Dam chose only to say others "perceived" him to be that way. This was not an accusation, just an observation of how other people felt. Furthermore, van Dam didn't say people were insulted or slighted or put off by Pausch's behavior. Instead, van Dam focused the results on Pausch; that it would limit what Pausch would accomplish in life. Not only that it would limit Pausch, but that it would be a shame, presumably because of all the talents Pausch had to offer.

All in all, this was a very gentle and skillful way to get Pausch to improve. Perhaps Pausch was able to think to himself: "Maybe others do perceive me that way, although surely I'm not that bad. After all I just want to be direct and effective. Well, maybe it is annoying to other people. Maybe it does hurt my chances of cooperating successfully with others. Maybe it is a shame I am so arrogant. I think I should change." Randy Pausch went on to affect the lives of many people before he died from pancreatic cancer in 2008.

It can be very tricky to tell someone in a diplomatic way that they need to make an improvement. If you're not sure you gave constructive feedback, you most likely didn't. Sometimes, even if you think you gave constructive feedback, it doesn't mean you did. Saying, "You should lose some weight," or, "You should quit smoking," or "You should do the project this way," is not constructive feedback. Those statements fall under the category of judgment and advice.

Imagine two people discussing a business idea. Let us take a look at the following responses:

"It sucks."

"It doesn't work."

"I've started several businesses and that's not going to work."

"The idea needs more work."

These comments are mostly negative, revealing few clues as to what is wrong.

"Your marketing plan doesn't work."

"You need a more detailed marketing plan."

The two comments above are still negative, but at least they're more specific."

"What is your marketing plan?"

"What's your SEO strategy?"

"That's a great idea! Now what's your marketing plan?"

"How else do you plan to market your business?"

Now we're moving into more exploratory and positive territory.

"You need to include social networking in your marketing plan."

"Can you add social networking to your marketing plan?"

"Social networking will give your business more reach."

"Social networking might give your business more reach."

"I think your idea solves an unaddressed problem for Internet users. Including social networks in your marketing could give your business even more reach."

Of all the different comments above, I think it is clear that most people would prefer to hear the last one. But what are the reasons? The comments above differ in a number of ways. Some are vague, whereas some are more precise. Obviously, the more precise the comment, the better. If I hear, "It doesn't work!" I don't know whether a portion or the whole thing is unsatisfactory. Some of the comments are orders. One is a request. If you're in a hurry or in a hierarchical situation, then orders can be very effective. If you want to promote engagement and foster discussion, then requests might be preferred. One question uses the acronym SEO (search engine optimization). If acronyms and technical terms are understood by everyone, they can be very effective. Otherwise, they just add to the confusion. Some phrases have more certainty or finality to them and tend to discourage further discussion. Some comments have a more aggressive tone; some are worded as subjective opinions. If I hear an aggressive comment, I might be provoked to defend my ideas. The last comment suggests a good approach and even starts off with some specific praise.

Generally speaking, when I encounter something for the first time, I might experience a gut reaction. It "feels good" or "looks wrong" or I don't feel particularly strongly about it. Then I have to make an effort to wrap words around my feelings to form a coherent thought that I can express. If I don't like something, I have to try to identify the flaw. Alternately, if I like something, I have to figure out what makes it work. Now I am ready to say that "the marketing plan isn't detailed enough," or "the business addresses a specific need." Next, I have to think about how the flaw might be fixed. Obviously, in this day and age, "we need to include social networking." Why? Because "social networking will give your business more reach." If I decide not to be as forceful with my opinion, I change the word "will" to "might." Making my opinion less forceful makes it a little easier for others to respond with their own ideas. Perhaps the idea to use social networking leads to another idea to advertise on targeted websites, which might be even better. And then, of course, I can lead off by giving some specific and positive feedback.

To come up with constructive feedback, first identify a strength and see if that strength is underused or if there is a better way to use it. Look for ways the situation can be made better. Look at the subject from different angles. How effective is the packaging, delivery, and marketing? Can it be made more well-rounded, more complete?

By couching your ideas in an easy tone, you let them speak for themselves. You're not crowding others out with the strength of your conviction, dismissiveness, intimidation, displays of authority, negativity, quick wit, sarcasm, excitement, arrogance, or other emotional displays. If you take pleasure in criticizing and finding flaws, then people have to improve despite your comments. Being an effective communicator isn't about how much experience you have. It isn't about exerting or displaying your authority. It isn't about showing off what you know. A good communicator has valuable ideas and knows how to express them effectively. By using the right tone, you are making it as easy as possible for someone to hear and entertain your ideas.

The important point is that you should offer something useful, as judged by the recipient. If you don't have any ideas to contribute, you can still assist in other ways. And by the way, if you feel you always have to shout to get your ideas across, then you have bigger problems. That could be a result of no one listening.

You want to avoid people thinking the following thoughts about you:

"She's always so bossy."
"He's so negative."
"He's always got an opinion."

You want people to come to you because: first, you listen to what they have to say. Second, you have valuable input. Third, you deliver that input in the most diplomatic and pleasant manner. It's better for morale if your subordinates don't want to avoid seeing you because you micro-manage. It's better if they don't feel forced to keep you in the loop and dread all the changes you will inevitably want. People feel less nervous if they don't have to constantly defend their decisions or argue about why they've done things a certain way. At home, the atmosphere is calmer when your kids aren't always expecting you to yell at them and tell them what they can and cannot do.

I'm not saying that you need to give constructive feedback all the time. But if this isn't in your toolkit, then you are missing a great way to make people want to come to you for your opinion. People really like constructive feedback. It can be easy on the ears, and easy on the ego. It can give you something specific that you can improve upon. You just have to do it once and people will respect your opinion and your tactfulness. If you're good at constructive feedback, you'll be the first person people turn to for help and advice.

Exercise—"Always Look on the Bright Side of Life"[§]

Come up with some comments about something and then label them as complaints, requests, demands, constructive, etc.

Is it easier to come up with complaints or is it easier to come up with constructive comments? Why?

Try to convert some of the complaints into constructive comments. For example:

"That lamp is ugly."

"You should change that lamp."

"A modern lamp style might blend in better with the rest of the room."

———

We have already mentioned specific praise while we were talking about constructive feedback. Praise, thank yous and apologies are much more meaningful and

---

[§]   Title of song written by Eric Idle. Originally featured in the 1979 film *Monty Python's Life of Brian*.

impactful when they are specific. Look at the following examples:

"Thanks," he said, barely looking away from his computer.

"Thank you," he said grudgingly.

"Thank you. Your offer was very gracious and it saved me a lot of trouble," he said, looking me in the eye and nodding.

"Sorry," he mumbled.

"I'm sorry I'm being forced to say, 'Sorry.'"

"I'm sorry I caused all that trouble. It was inconsiderate of me."

As we all know, you can use the words, "great," "thank you," and "sorry" for utterly sarcastic purposes. Vague praise is open to interpretation. "He said he liked it." "She said it was good." Did he say he liked it just to be polite, or does he have some other agenda? What exactly did he like? If you are not specific when you praise someone, you lose an opportunity to build good will and differentiate yourself as someone who notices things and is rewarding to work with. To give specific praise, you have to pay attention to what is happening. Was the effort commendable? Was the result pleasing, original, creative, thorough, or worthy of praise in some other way?

Exercise—Go Watch TV and Get on the Internet

Try to come up with some specific praise for your favorite television program or movie or sports game. Be as specific and use as many adjectives as possible. Go on the Forum section of my website www.8StepListen.com. Are people listening to one another? Are people acknowledging what has been said in previous posts, or are they more concerned about making their own points and being heard? How would you keep things positive and add value with your input?

———————

EXAMPLES

To illustrate the points in this chapter, let us look at some examples. Mike is preparing for an important presentation. He decides to ask Sarah for some assistance.

"Why don't you set the context and then go through your presentation once?" suggests Sarah.

Right from the beginning, Sarah sets the tone. No presentation or story exists in a vacuum and Sarah makes sure she gets the background information she needs. Her request for the context gives Mike confidence in her sincere interest. Mike explains the context and then proceeds with his presentation.

"That was good," says Sarah. "I liked the way you listed the options and then went into detail about the pros and cons of each. That was very thorough."

Sarah makes sure her praise is specific, which conveys to Mike that his hard work is noticed and appreciated.

"I did make a couple of notes. It seems there was a jump before the middle section," says Sarah.

"Yes, you're right," Mike agrees. "I noticed a disconnect myself when I was going through it. Let me make a note so I can fix it later."

Because he had a listener, Mike had to deliver the presentation in a logically coherent way, with a beginning, middle and end. Simply by listening, Sarah functioned as a sounding board and helped Mike uncover a disconnect. Sarah was very tactful in her comment, "It seems there was a jump," and it created an opening for discussion. In effect, she asked Mike, "Do you agree?" If Mike had disagreed, Sarah could have asked Mike to repeat that section so both of them could assess if there was a logical gap.

Under different circumstances, Sarah may have advised Mike differently. Mike could have said at the beginning, "I don't do a lot of presentations. Just tell me how to fix things. I don't want to spend a lot of time on it." In this case, Sarah might have said, "You need to add a slide here." Or, "You need a better transition there." She would be providing a fix and identifying a flaw. She'd be advising and giving instructions.

Meanwhile, Sarah continues with the discussion of Mike's presentation.

"What is your final recommendation?" Sarah asks.

"I'm not sure," admits Mike. "It depends on my manager's input. The last time he had a clear preference. But things have changed because of the economy. That's why I didn't include anything in the presentation. You know what? I think I'll ask my manager and then update the presentation based on his answer."

By asking a good question, Sarah allowed Mike to talk about his reasoning. Sarah may have realized that the ending to Mike's presentation lacked impact. After talking it out, Mike was then able to come up with a solution himself. If Mike had not come up with the idea to consult with his manager, Sarah could also have suggested it.

"You have a lot of good material here. I think you're more prepared than you thought you were," says Sarah.

"You're right. I feel much better about the presentation now. Thanks for the comments and the help."

Sarah wraps things up by reminding Mike of his thorough preparations and suggests that he need not be nervous. She highlights the positive to encourage Mike.

For our next example, let us drop in on a wife who is in the middle of redecorating her living room. She's looked at a number of carpets. She's brought back some swatches and is laying them on the floor to see how they might look in the room. She asks her husband, "What do you think?"

The husband is caught off guard. Interior design and decorations are not his thing. He would be perfectly happy with his wife making all the decisions. In fact, he would prefer it.

"Whatever you pick is fine," he says.

"Yes, but what do you think? I'd like your input," replies the wife.

The wife may have worked hard on the selections. She might want her husband to make a genuine effort to participate and to assist. It may not be enough for the husband to offer quick suggestions or snap judgments. But what if the husband really doesn't know his way around carpets? In this case, the husband might choose either to spend time to study his wife's carpet selections, or as an alternative help her with other housework so she can concentrate on the carpets. These actions allow the husband to recognize his wife's hard work. In the end, you can't force someone to contribute, nor should you ignore a request for assistance.

How about a different story:

"Honey, the only clean shirt I have is pink. What tie should I wear with it?"

The wife goes through the tie rack and helps the husband pick out something that doesn't clash.

Moments later, the husband emerges with a different tie; a green one. The wife gives the husband an exasperated look.

"What?" says the husband, "I like the dollar signs on this tie!"

What is the point of the last story? Perhaps the lesson is to be prepared to be asked to be a contributor, but don't always expect people to act on your suggestions or input.

SUMMARY

The whole purpose of being a contributor is to add something to a conversation without distracting from the topic or taking it over completely. In some ways, listening as a contributor is like being a good waiter, or being like a gracious party host.

Here are some tips for being a better conversation contributor:

1. Get the background information if it is needed. "What stage are we at?"
2. Ask good questions to get the speaker to elaborate or clarify thoughts and confusing or missing items.
3. Encourage the speaker to talk things out by being a sounding board. You might ask for a step-by-step overview of the entire plan, or specific details of one part of the plan.
4. Help people find better words to describe what is happening in their lives.
5. Give specific praise so the speaker knows exactly what worked.
6. Make it easy for your feedback to be heard and leave the door open for further discussion. Offer your ideas and suggestions in a constructive fashion.
7. Give instructions and identify problems, if appropriate.

Being a good contributor makes you rewarding to work. It makes you a more effective parent and manager. Instead of doling out your opinions whether people want it or not, your wisdom will be sought after.

Chapter 7 Cool, Calm, Caring, Clever Counselor

"Oh, the comfort - the inexpressible comfort of feeling *safe* with a person - having neither to weigh thoughts nor measure words, but to pour them all out, just as they are, chaff and grain together; certain that a faithful hand will take and sift them, keep what is worth keeping, and then with the breath of kindness blow the rest away."
Dinah Craik

Imagine a friend telling you one of the following. What would you do?

"We just lost the lawsuit to hold on to the patent of our most profitable product."

"They fired me! Just like that!"

"We have a crisis on our hands!"

"I've been training for a year, but I still don't know if I'm ready to run a marathon!"

"My boyfriend hit me again, but he was so sorry afterward."

123

Sometimes in life we encounter difficulties and setbacks. These could be a result of external factors— man-made or natural—or they could be a result of our own expectations and desires not being met. Sometimes we have doubts about whether we can achieve our goals, or we have doubts about those around us. When this happens, we feel sad, angry, disappointed, or frustrated. If we know what needs to be done, we can resolve the situation. If not, then we feel unsure and confused. We feel paralyzed. We worry that we will never solve the problem.

We might understand our options intellectually. We know we can appeal an unfavorable patent ruling or move on. We know we can either continue our marathon training or stop. What we don't know is the ultimate costs and results of these options. We have genuine doubts and concerns. Or we postpone the tough decisions we know we have to make. In a novel situation, we might be caught off guard and not have any previous experience to guide us. We might not even know what options and actions are available to us.

A counselor can really help a person during uncertain times. When we listen to others as counselors, we bring compassion, objectivity and problem-solving skills and wrap them all up with good listening. We acknowledge the confusion and frustration of the situation. This gives the other person a chance to settle down a little, emotionally[24]. We allow, and in fact encourage, the other person to talk about different aspects of the issue. We help people think through their situations more objectively from start to finish. We help others understand and come to terms with what has happened. We act as a sounding board. We ask journalistic questions so people can understand the full story. We help by asking basic questions about the issue at hand. When it is time to think about possible solutions, we look for creative ways to get past or resolve issues. We ask questions to explore options. We help people approach problems in a healthier, more productive manner. By healthier, I mean an approach that neither surrenders to nor robs control or dignity from someone else. A counselor helps people help themselves.

COMFORT THE DISTRESSED

I once tried to get a number of things done during a trip. Because I didn't have a lot of time to complete the tasks, I felt under pressure. I got into fights with people and became quite frustrated. At the time, I spoke to my friends about what was happening. One friend kept asking me about all the things I'd tried to resolve the problems. After a while I got tired of justifying my actions. Another friend didn't know what to say and started talking about some of her own experiences in similar situations. This unfortunately prevented me from finding a solution to my problems.

The kicker is I didn't even realize how frustrated I was until days after I returned from my trip. I was standing in line at the supermarket, I was tired of waiting, and I felt myself growing increasingly impatient and agitated. That's when I realized how frustrated I was. When I got home, I thought about what was bothering me. I wrote down the list of things I'd wanted to do on that trip, and I saw that I'd failed to complete several tasks. I felt I was held back by circumstances out of my control, which added to the frustration. Getting into fights and exchanging words with others didn't help, either. In the end, I simply accepted that I didn't have enough time to do everything, and I decided to look for alternative ways to follow up on the incomplete items. Once I got to that point, I was able to calm down.

Sometimes we can be upset about something for a long time without knowing exactly how upset we are or why we are upset. "I'm so angry I want to throw something!" If someone is overwhelmed, help her realize she may be trying to do too many things at once. If she is frustrated, she might be trying to force something to happen. When you listen as a counselor, you use your empathy to help the other person get in touch with emotions, to offer him safety to give in to his feelings. Be patient with him. Let him know it is okay to feel sad, angry, or frightened. Let her sob, clench her fists, or be frightened. Again, just describing the feelings can have a calming effect. Reassure him that he doesn't have to go through these feelings alone.

A note of caution: because of the raw nature of the feelings, you do have to be careful. There is no right or wrong way to help. Everyone brings her or his own combination of skills and preferences to the table. Even if you do everything "right," your actions can still be misunderstood as intrusive or inappropriate. The only thing you can do is check in as you go along and apologize if there is any misunderstanding.

HELP WITH THE PRESENT

A few years ago I had to make a decision to move to another city. I wasn't happy with my job and I needed a change. And yet I wasn't prepared to make a big move. For several months I went back and forth about my choices, unable—or perhaps unwilling—to make a decision. "Maybe things will change at work." "It's hopeless here. I can't wait forever!" The pending decision hung over my head. I would tell my friends out of frustration, "I'm going to leave and never work with this stuff again!" When I finally made my decision and moved, the fog lifted.

When someone is going through a tough decision, you can certainly help come up with a list of pros and cons. But until he is ready to decide, you may simply have to watch patiently as he changes his mind back and forth. He might talk about making rash moves out of frustration. You have to use your judgment to determine whether he is just frustrated and needs to vent a little, or whether he really intends to do something in haste. If you say, "Oh, you're just frustrated," you might sound like you're minimizing his feelings. Always listen to others seriously.

Occasionally, people don't feel they have the time to process their emotions. I was talking to a friend during lunch one day. Her father had just passed away[25]. She was too busy with her job and taking care of two young children to give herself the time to mourn. She was fighting back the tears and wanted to change the subject when I asked about her father. As a friend, you can suggest the other person take some time off. You can offer to help out with baby-sitting or picking the kids up from school or anything at all. A small gesture of kindness and thoughtfulness can mean a lot when offered during a crisis. One of my managers, Gregg Davis, once offered to give me his airline miles to make a trip back home following a family emergency. It was a very generous and gracious offer and I made sure I told everyone about his kindness. Even if you don't end up helping, the fact that you offered might prompt your friend to realize that she needs some time for herself. Your friend should also take care of herself before taking care of others. As they say on airplanes, you should put on your own oxygen mask before assisting others. You need to take care of your own emotional needs before you can really take care of others.

If someone is going through a chaotic situation, try to introduce certainty and clarity to the process. Now is probably not the time to share all the new and exciting things happening in your life. Plan a meeting in advance, or a series of activities. Touch base with them every now and again. Your efforts will create a sense of dependability and constancy. In terms of bringing clarity to a chaotic situation, a simple thing to do is to suggest or help them take notes. Write down the things that are known and the things that are not known. Keep notes of things as they develop.

You can also help people deflect nosy questions from outsiders. People like to look at traffic accidents. In fact, nowadays people like to slow down their cars enough so that they can take pictures of accidents with their cell phone cameras. Accidents are unusual and each one is unique. We're shocked each time at how solid metal can be twisted and mangled by crash forces. We're curious if anyone was hurt. Seeing the wreckage at an accident also makes us feel better about following traffic rules. Similarly, people are sometimes curious about other people's troubles. The troubles of your friend are not raw material for the entertainment and amusement for others. My favorite way to deal with nosy people is to let them use their own imaginations to entertain themselves.

"Did you yell at him?" asks the nosy guy.
"I had a good talk with him."
"C'mon! Tell me!" urges the nosy guy.
"I had a good talk with him."
"I knew it! You let him have it, didn't you?"
"I had a good talk with him."

The nosy guy is looking for exciting gossip. Neither confirm nor deny his probing guesses. Eventually, he will realize that your answers are nowhere as sensational and interesting as he would like them to be and he will go away.

I once was trying to help a friend. Unfortunately, in the middle, I grew tired and upset and basically told her she could do whatever she wanted. I apologized later, but she still remembers the sting of being abandoned during her time of need. Once you commit to helping someone, you have to do your best to be supportive and encouraging. Be mentally prepared, because your patience might be stretched thin if your friend sinks into despair and you grow tired of your "helpful ideas and wonderful advice" being ignored. If you really can't help, make sure someone else is there to take over for you.

Sometimes, to get past a current situation, we have to stretch ourselves a little. As listeners we can sometimes help others to challenge the assumptions behind self-imposed limitations. I used to have a colleague who confessed that he didn't know much about investing. He said it was too difficult. Then one day I overheard him explaining his favorite fantasy sports in detail to someone else. He talked about statistics, strategy, planning and luck. So I told him investing had many similarities to his favorite hobby. "You look at past performance, you have an investment strategy, you plan and you need a bit of luck. You're so good at your hobby. You study it, you work at it, you read books about it. It proves you have the ability and the aptitude to do these things."

Similarly, my mother can tell you all kinds of stories about the community, but I have to persuade her to devote even part of her vast memory to learning how to operate "all that technology stuff". Sometimes we have pre-conceived notions about areas where we are lacking. "I've never been good at math." "I've never been artistic." "I've never been outspoken or good at public speaking." We let these thoughts convince us that we are doomed to failure and we discount any evidence that would indicate otherwise. We don't realize we can take skills in one area of life and apply them to another. We aren't always used to viewing the hard work and dedication we put into our hobbies and daily chores as accomplishments and strengths. We just like our hobbies. We just like spending time on learning more and honing our skills at our favorite pastimes. We don't always want to think that with work and dedication, we can often embrace change and new things. Of course it is a different thing to say that you are much more interested in sports than in investing. It is also different to say you haven't come across a book or teacher that made investing interesting to you. Those are acceptable reasons for not liking something. But it isn't always accurate to assume that you're not good at something and to use that as an excuse for not trying.

When helping someone, make sure you are available and follow up. Think of yourself as a good salesperson. Until the issues have been resolved (the sale is closed or the contract signed), you should try to be available to your friend. I had a friend who one day called me up out of the blue. She was feeling particularly low about her life. She asked if I could meet her to talk. I could and I did. I tried to listen to her as a counselor, and it seemed I helped her.

My friend dropped out of sight for some time and I didn't hear from her. I tried gently to inquire about her current status. I didn't want to micromanage her progress, but to let her know that her progress was worthy of my, and hence her own, attention.

Several years ago, I found myself listening to a friend while we sat in a park. My friend started crying while we were talking. It was a late summer afternoon and people were walking by us. Towards the end of the conversation, when she had recovered from her despair, I made the following joke:

"You can cry… just don't slap me across the face and walk away as if I just broke your heart!"

My friend laughed. Even though someone might be upset, you can still remind them that there is humor and laughter. You can remind them that life still goes on. Of course, you shouldn't attempt humor or any other kind of distraction while the other person is still working through their emotions.

PLAN FOR THE FUTURE

I know people who have remained at unhappy jobs for years before finally leaving. The idea of looking for another job and starting over again seems too much to handle. Instead, they come up with a list of concerns and excuses to justify their reluctance to look. "Will the commute be worse?" "I'll have to give up my hard-earned seniority." "I'll look for a job when the economy improves." Try to steer your friend away from worrying about things out of his or her control. You should certainly take sensible precautions against risks. Beyond that, it may not be worth it for your friend to obsess and worry. For example, you can wash your hands before touching your face, you should always wear a seatbelt, but it isn't practical never to leave the house. Change always comes with a certain amount of risk. A lot of times we just wish the current, familiar situation would improve on its own. We postpone taking any steps to risk something completely new. In these cases, you first have to acknowledge the difficulty in making a change. Be just as honest about the real risks as well as the real rewards. Help the other person minimize or deal with the real risks and help him keep an eye on the benefits. Then, you can help by breaking the overwhelming task down into smaller ones.

"I understand it isn't easy to find a good job. It can be a lot of work, and you have to take rejection in stride. On the other hand, there could be a lot of benefits."

"Why don't you just update your resume this weekend? That's all. Can you do that?"

"Why don't you just answer one job advertisement this week? You can turn them down if it doesn't work out."

"Why don't you answer three advertisements every month?"

Remember to set deadlines and be encouraging when the smaller tasks are completed.

Another avoidance mechanism people sometimes use is they try to minimize the problem. They try to resign themselves to their misfortune. "My job isn't that bad. I can still manage." The point isn't whether your friend can still manage under the difficult situation. Not everything is an endurance contest. The point is your friend can do better. Your friend can be more successful and productive at another job, regardless of her current situation. Remind him of the positive benefits of a new job. "You can pay off your credit card debt. You can afford a new car with a bigger paycheck. You've always wanted more responsibility. You can make better use of your talents." Remind him of the positive qualities he can bring to a better job.

Most people aren't good at tasks they don't do on a regular basis. As listeners, we need to be sensitive to this. Unfamiliar tasks may include things like asking for a raise, interviewing, self-promotion, breaking up, making big, life-changing decisions, talking about emotions, and sharing weaknesses. Unfortunately, we often have to do things outside of our comfort zone in order to overcome difficulties. Again, if it were easy and routine, we would have already fixed the problem. It's perfectly normal to be a little frightened or nervous about making positive changes. Once your friend accepts that she's nervous or anxious, she can take steps to deal with it. You can help her look for information on the web. You can help her rehearse and practice interviewing. Try to help your friend make better decisions from a position of greater confidence. If a job is worth doing, if a change is worth making, then it's worth doing it right. If she really doesn't have time to address the issue fully, that's fine too, as long as she appreciates later on that she had to operate under time constraints. When she resolves the problem, she can celebrate the fact that it always takes a certain amount of courage to move forward.

That brings me to another point. Improvements and changes have to be made at each person's own pace. What is effortless and easy for some can be tricky and frustrating for others. A friend of mine got upset with me once because she felt I wasn't doing enough to look for a job. She would listen to me complain and offer ideas, which I would never use. It's not that I disagreed with her ideas. I'm sure I would be a more successful person if I was better at networking, job hunting, and self-promotion. I sensed her frustration at my lack of movement on the job front. "I know you feel I'm not living up to my potential. But I hate marketing myself (or asking for raises, more responsibilities, etc.) You can teach me how to do it. You can help me enjoy doing it. Just please don't get frustrated with me or make me feel inadequate or stupid in the process."

Whether someone needs to be prodded or coaxed into doing something for themselves really depends on the situation. If someone is still feeling very emotional about a situation, then you probably want to take a more comforting approach. If they are dragging their feet and not making progress, you might need to be more firm. Sometimes, you have to do both in a sensible combination!

My friend tried to remind me of my strengths to give me more confidence to start networking. She reminded me of my achievements and accomplishments. "You've already practically been running the department for a year. And didn't you say you feel more energetic since you started making more decisions?" She tried to help me find creative options to solve my problem. She helped me look toward a better future, as opposed to just cutting or minimizing loss. As counselors, we can help our friends, family members and colleagues look for better options, and help them avoid blindly quitting a lousy job or relationship and rushing into something equally or more problematic. Most importantly, we can encourage our friends to find their own solutions. Ultimately, it is their life and their decision and their responsibility.

KNOW WHEN TO STOP

Now that we have seen some of the things we can do as a counselor, let us look at some of the things we should try to avoid. While you are being as helpful and considerate as you can, you don't want to encourage dependency. You're not just a nice person who will listen indefinitely as the other person gets into the habit of complaining and lamenting without making changes or improvements. And even though listening is first and foremost about helping others, you must make sure you don't get frustrated in the process. Your colleague's situation itself may be very frustrating or difficult. Perhaps you're dealing with an abused spouse with little financial independence. She may not be willing or able to receive monetary assistance. Perhaps it is a substance abuser who hasn't hit bottom yet. You, yourself, may be tired or unsure about what to do. There are many, many valid reasons why you may not be able to help those who come to you for listening. The wisest thing to do in this case is to step back. Do your very best to encourage your friend to talk to another trusted advisor or seek professional help.

Exercise—Good Samaritan

Do you know someone who has set a personal goal for themselves? For example, learn to play the guitar, exercise more, start a business, pass a professional exam, etc.? How can you provide support and encouragement to that person?

Do you know someone who has encountered some difficulties? How can you provide support and encouragement to them?

———————

LISTEN TO YOURSELF

One advantage of talking to yourself is that you know at least somebody's listening.
Franklin P. Jones

Throughout this book, I have talked about putting someone else's needs ahead of your own. Now, finally, it's all about you! A lot of the skills that apply to external listening can actually be turned inward in a very useful, reflective way.

One of the biggest influences in my life was my English teacher. Not only did he listen to me, but he also managed to instill in me a love of language. But what I want to mention here is that he told our class to keep a journal (one page a day) and to write our memoirs. Writing your memoir (doesn't matter how young or how old you are) and keeping a journal is like getting to know your own past and writing about your present. A little bit of honest examination can give you a better perspective on your concerns, aspirations and relationships. It allows you to think more clearly about your future. It can be fun. It can help you sort out problems. You might even learn a thing or two about yourself, and when you reread what you wrote you might find that you may have changed or not changed in some unexpected ways over the years.

Think about the times when you were caught up with emotion. Think about an incident when you wanted to cry or hit someone. How did you get to where you are? Are you still afraid of the same things you were afraid of? How did you get started on some of your hobbies? What, if anything, makes them important to you? How did you end up in the profession you're in? What exactly do you think about family, about marriage, about love? I don't mean just generic statements such as "family is important". What makes it important? Is it because you know each other's histories? What do you think about your parents? Do you think they did the best they could, given their circumstances? What constructive feedback would you give them? If you have difficulties with your own children, does it change how you view your own parents? What constructive feedback would you give to a younger version of yourself? How do you spend money? Are you thrifty, or carefree? Why do you spend money the way you do? If you were to become more successful, would it change your answers to these questions?

As a side-benefit of my own journal-writing efforts, some of the more interesting things people think I have said off the cuff were actually things written down ahead of time. When I write things down, I can craft the sentences and edit the wording as much as I like. When I say it, people don't know how much work I put into it days before. Keeping a journal makes me appear smarter and more articulate!

What mistakes have you made in the past? I have broken things and then tried to return them to stores. I have yelled at people because I couldn't get my email. During college hazing, I found myself offering little resistance to loud orders to crawl around the floor and to insult other students. I have cut off other drivers and made other mistakes on the road. In other words, I know firsthand how easy it is to succumb to greed, peer pressure, temptation, carelessness and many other things. Keeping this in mind helps me appreciate how easy it is to make mistakes. It reminds me to be a little less judgmental than I would be otherwise.

When you encounter something frustrating, are you able to listen to yourself and calm yourself down? When you encounter difficulties, are you able to ask yourself the tough questions you need to ask? What is important to you? Where do you derive your sense of self? What achievements are you most proud of? Is your sense of self-worth grounded in an honest and fair assessment of who you are? Do you wonder about things? Do you have a sense of curiosity? Do you wonder why other people do the things they do? When faced with disappointment, do you blame yourself? Do you accept your lot in life, or do you explore and try new things? What are the most hurtful insults to you and why?

As a listener, it's always helpful if you have done the honest introspection in which you're asking the speaker to engage. If you're going to suggest the speaker entertain new ideas and new ways of doing things so that he can move past his current situation, then it helps if you have some experience with that, too. These are excellent reminders of the courage it takes sometimes to make changes.

YOU NEVER LISTEN

Now that you have looked at how you can serve someone by being an audience, a contributor, and a counselor, let us look at something you might hear in an argument: "You never listen!" The phrase easily evokes an image of a frustrated wife trying to get through to a clueless husband, or a defiant teenager pitted against well-intentioned but strict parents, or an angry parent yelling at a child. When we examine the phrase, we see that it doesn't really give much indication as to how the speaker's needs are not being met. Does the speaker have a story to tell? Is the speaker looking for some help to sort things out? What exactly is the speaker upset about? If you cannot clearly explain your frustration to the other party, then how can he or she make the necessary adjustments?

The next time you feel the urge to exclaim, "You never listen", you might be better served by instead choosing from one of the following:

1) You never let me tell or finish my stories.
   Because:
   You don't pay full attention.
   You interrupt.
   You try to one-up my story.
   You correct the way I tell my story.
   You try to improve my story.
   You make jokes instead of listen.

2) You never help me talk through things or work with me cooperatively on ideas.
   Because:
   You try to take over or take control.
   You keep giving me suggestions to the point where I lose interest in my own ideas.
   You start giving suggestions before you even know where I want your input.
   You don't give me any input or feedback.
   You don't take my ideas seriously.

3) I never want to talk to you if I have a crisis—and I'm having one now!
   Because:
   You don't understand how upset I am.
   You don't make me feel better.
   Your string of suggestions makes me feel like I haven't tried hard enough.
   You try to solve my problem while I'm still upset.
   You make me tired of answering your questions.

EXAMPLES

Our first example involves listening to ourselves in a situation fraught with uncertainty and anxiety. Back in late 1999, the world was concerned with the Y2K problem—the fear that critical computer systems might fail on New Year's Eve 2000. At that time, I was working at an investment bank. We had plans for Y2K. We had rehearsals to go through emergency procedures. We also had meetings to discuss the issues. At the end of one town hall meeting, they opened the floor for questions. I raised my hand and asked one of the senior managers, "What's your greatest fear?" I was hoping for some kind of insight. I thought perhaps he could tell us something interesting because of his senior position in the company and in the industry. But all I remember was that his answer was vague. I left the meeting with an empty feeling.

Over the next few days, I thought about my question. I asked myself, "What exactly did I want him to say?" I kept asking myself questions and I slowly began to piece things together. I used my questioning techniques. "What is the worst that can happen?" "What is the best case scenario?" "What are the risks that we face?" "What have we done to mitigate those risks?" "What would happen if we cannot mitigate them?"

Eventually I found the answers to those questions. I finally understood that I actually had a number of concerns and fears, and that they were the root cause of my anxiety. So if I asked the question again, "What's your greatest fear?" this is the answer I would have liked to hear:

"The worse that could happen is that civilization as we know it could come to an end. But that isn't necessarily going to happen. There is a good chance that Y2K could in fact turn out to be a big yawn! We have spent lots of money and personnel resources over the last few months and years fixing this problem. We have fixed all the problems that we can find. We have had rehearsals. We have learned from our rehearsals. We are prepared for this."

"There will always be problems that we cannot possibly anticipate or that are out of our control. If anything unexpected happens, I want you folks to stay calm. Go through the procedures you have been given. I am confident that I can count on the resourcefulness of our staff to resolve any unexpected problems as they come up. You are all among the best at what you do. That's why we hired you."

Now why would I choose to say that if I were in the manager's position? First, I acknowledge people's fears. A lot of times we don't understand our fears. We don't know they are there or we don't know what exactly it is we are afraid of. There is a sense of unease or anxiety that we can't put a finger on. By correctly identifying it, we make it more tangible and less frightening. Or at least there is less of a tendency to get hysterical about it.

Second, I put it in perspective. It doesn't have to be a doomsday scenario. In hindsight, we all know Y2K was by and large uneventful, but at the time, it would have helped if someone had reminded us of that possibility. By stating a positive outcome, it also gives people hope and something to look forward to. They don't have to be fixated or overwhelmed by negative thoughts only.

Third, I reassure people by informing them of the remediation steps that have been taken. Sometimes in a big company, you don't know what everybody else is doing. I'm reassuring the staff that no money and effort was spared to fix all the known problems. I'm also stating that "we are prepared". When people are confused, they want their leaders to show confidence. They want to know that their leaders can see a way out.

Fourth, I remind people of the fact that we cannot anticipate everything. Y2K was truly unprecedented. But that doesn't mean that we have to panic at the first sign of any unexpected problem.

Finally, I make them feel good about themselves. People say investment banks hire the best and the brightest. I remind them of that and I appeal to their resourcefulness to pull us through.

The second example, perhaps fittingly, involves the creation of this book. The process of writing this book has certainly had its ups and down. Colleagues expressed polite amusement when they heard I was going to take time off to write it. Friends told me to stick to my day job. When I was doing well, I would run into the streets with my head full of ideas. When I encountered obstacles, I would question my own sanity, the odds of ever getting published and read, and whether it was all worth it. Throughout this adventure, my girlfriend was always supportive and encouraging.

She kept her doubts to herself. She was always available to listen to my latest ideas and writing problems. She listened to my concerns, yet never allowed them to overwhelm me. When I had doubts, she would remind me of my strengths and the things I had already accomplished. She did little things like buy me books on listening, and she talked to her friends about my project. She was always supportive and encouraging and she always listened.

SUMMARY

When something bad happens and we don't know which way to turn, there are only a few things we can do. We have to count on our basic values such as integrity, honesty, fairness, and common sense to guide us. A counselor brings those basic values as well as support and encouragement to the friend, family member, colleague and others in need.

Here are a few final tips for being a good counselor:

1. Be patient. Try to be committed to helping.
2. Be an attentive audience.
3. Help the other person in the present. Empathize with their loss and disappointment.
4. Help describe the uncertainty. What are the worst-case and best-case scenarios? What is the most likely scenario?
5. Remind them of their strengths and accomplishments.
6. Follow up.
7. Remind them of humor and other small pleasures of life.
8. Help them explore different options.
9. Help them plan for the future.
10. Help them overcome excuses.

By being organized, you show stability just when people don't know where to turn. By being wise, you provide insight just when people are lost and confused. By being compassionate, you show others how to let go and move on. Don't let fear lead the other person to confusion and hopelessness. Don't let fear drive them to the other extreme of hatred and anger either. Let justice and fairness, wisdom, and compassion guide their thoughts and actions. Help them use the challenges to be a better person.

Chapter 8 You Listen to Me!

"…I really wish I'd listened to what my mother told me when I was young."
"Why, what did she tell you?"
"I don't know, I didn't listen."
Douglas Adams

Real life is messy. It's where the chaos hits the fan. People make mistakes, tempers flare, sparks fly. Fortunately, we don't have to accept this state of affairs as inevitable. By looking at some common mistakes, and by analyzing how anger can escalate, we can look for ways to work around or circumvent the trouble spots.

And then there's listening in the corporate world. In commercials, companies that want to project a caring, service-oriented image like to talk about how they listen. In this chapter, we'll dig a little deeper and look at some of the real decisions that need to be made to improve listening in businesses.

STOP THAT!

Everybody knows kids can't sit still. I was riding the subway one day. On the same subway train was a father and his young child. The child started swinging around one of the poles in the train.

"Stop that!" the father said.

The child stopped swinging around the pole. Moments later, the child started again.

"Stop doing that!" the father repeated.

The child stopped. A few minutes later, the child was swinging again.

"When mommy and I say something, you have to listen!"

What is going on here? Do our poor habits of listening start from childhood and simply get worse over time? Why do we ignore advice that we know is good for us?

It turns out there are quite a few things happening here. First of all, when the father reminded his son to listen, what he really meant was, "When mommy and I give you an order, you must obey!" The word "listen," in English and in other languages, can mean to hear or to obey. Yes, parents make requests for the benefit of their children. But when the wording is changed, the cautious admonition of a father suddenly turns into a rigid and authoritarian command. Instead of hearing useful advice, the child feels he is being bossed around. And because none of us like to be forced to obey commands all the time, we look for the first opportunity to disobey.

Now let's see what happens next:

"When mommy and I say something, you have to listen!" said the father.

"I did listen. And then I got bored again," replied the child.

"Well, then you didn't listen," said the father.

What if the child had responded, "I heard you. I considered your order. I obeyed. And then I got bored again!" Now we see that the child has his own priorities and needs. Most children cannot sit still for a long time because they get bored.

What if the father had said, "Are you bored? Would you like me to tell you a story?" This directly addresses the child's needs and gives him an appealing alternative. Or perhaps the father could have patiently explained, "Son, I know you are bored, but this is not a playground. The train is moving and you can lose your balance and get hurt. There are other people on this train and you might accidentally hit someone."

What if the father had said this instead: "You can play on two conditions. One, if you fall down, you must not cry. Two, if you hit someone else or get in someone else's way, you have to stop and apologize. Promise?" In this case, the father is pointing out the possible consequences of his child's actions and asking the child to take responsibility for his own choices.

This simple example clearly shows a number of things can and often do go wrong in our communications. We confuse requests with commands. We ignore other people's needs. We don't talk about things in a precise fashion. We're not clear about our wishes and the reasons behind those wishes.

I once had to apply for a travel visa. I gathered all my documents, and headed to the embassy. However, as soon as I arrived and presented my paperwork to the clerk in the waiting room, I was told I had to make an appointment. She stabbed a finger at the instructions on one of my letters. I was told I had to come back another day.

In desperation I said, "Can you make an exception please?"

The moment I said it, I regretted it, because she raised her voice and said, "No exceptions!" Then she went on about the rules and how she would have to make exceptions for everyone else. It was as if all her training as a civil servant consisted of denying exceptions.

I walked out to the elevator lobby and wondered how I could have been so careless and not read the instructions completely. I waited for the elevator, not sure what I was going to do next.

I decided to try again, since I had nothing to lose. I went back into the office and walked up to the clerk's desk. I said to her in a calm voice, "I know it is my mistake, I know I'm not supposed to be here today. But it would..." I hesitated as I thought about what I wanted to say. "It would make things a lot easier for me if I could do this today."

She went away for a moment. When she came back, she said that the officer would see me. I saw the officer, handed in my paperwork and answered some very routine questions. In a few minutes, it was all done. I walked back out to the waiting room. I was angry that the woman had given me such a hard time earlier. But I decided to swallow my anger. I turned towards her and said, "Thank you," and left the room.

I stood there waiting for the elevator again. I was relieved that I got everything done and I could head back home. Suddenly, the clerk came out to the lobby and said, "I didn't want to stop you earlier. It was the officer who didn't want to see you." I thanked her again and she went back into the office.

A lot of times when we need something, we do a poor job of explaining why we need the assistance. We state our needs without any justification, and our requests often sound like orders and demands. When we feel we are right about something, we use a tone that suggests superiority on our part, while implying guilt on the other. "Close the fridge! Don't waste electricity! Stop doing that!" "I'm right and you're wrong!" When we do this, we are actually taking other people for granted, or forcing them to defend their actions. Or our well-intentioned advice turns into nagging orders. Instead, another approach is first to acknowledge that we're the ones that have a need, or acknowledge that we screwed up, if that's the case. If we feel we're right, we can take a little more time to explain our positions. If we can patiently and clearly explain our reasons more often, then we have a better chance of getting agreement when we don't have the time to explain. Once we have done that, then we can ask for assistance and cooperation. Instead of expecting help, commanding people or forcing people to defend their positions, appeal to their desire to help. And when everything is done, thank them.

One time, my Internet connection developed problems. The connection would drop completely a few times a minute. I emailed customer support and described the situation. A few days later, they sent me back a very pleasant email. It began by addressing me as "Dear Mr. / Mrs. Wong." They thanked me for contacting them. They confirmed my complaint by paraphrasing it back to me, "I understand that you find it difficult to get connected to the Internet". Next, they admitted that it was a known issue. Unfortunately, they were not able to tell me when the problem would be fixed. However, they reassured me that they were "diligently working on it." I was told I'd be given an update. I was given some support phone numbers, a link to frequently asked support questions, and I was even asked to "Please take a moment to fill out a customer satisfaction survey."

A week later, I was still having problems with my Internet connection. And I hadn't had an update from my service provider. I contacted customer support again. How could they not have an estimate on how long it would take to fix the problem? Was it a serious problem, or was it a small issue with a quick fix? Each time I dealt with a new support person, I had to explain the situation from scratch and go through the same inconclusive troubleshooting steps. These big companies all have lousy support. The right hand never knows what the left hand is doing!

What happened to me being a "valued customer"? What happened to all the advertised claims of speed and reliability and good customer service? Now that something was wrong, all those claims seemed like lies! I had to do something. I had to ratchet up the rhetoric and start making some demands!

In the end, I finally stumbled upon the right person who knew what needed to be done. A technician was dispatched to my home and the problem was fixed.

When we analyze this story, we can see how an ordinary problem can quickly deteriorate into a full shouting match. Something disagreeable happens and we voice our objection. We get a standard response, or the other side states that things are under control. After a while, if things don't change, we start wondering what happened. We start thinking that it is unfair. We think about all the things we should get and all the things we should not have to do to get it. We think about all the previous times we've been disappointed. We justify our expectations. Worse, we justify our frustration and anger. We resort to cheap stereotypes instead of making the effort to search for reasonable reasons for other people's behavior. "These large companies all have lousy support!" The more angry we are, the more inconsiderate and thoughtless the other side must be. We obviously need to raise our voices and take more dramatic action to get heard! Let's go on the offense! The nerve! The other side defends and fights back!

Where do these three stories take us? Even well-intentioned teachings from a father are not always accurate or address the full complexity of a situation. When we need something from others, we don't always do a good job asking. When things go wrong, we contrast our high expectations with the imperfect reality to justify our frustration and resulting outbursts. We get impatient and we get upset. We are oh-so-human and we make mistakes all along the way.

EVERYBODY STAY CALM!

In modern society, fortunately or unfortunately, there's one area where it is recognized that mistakes and carelessness are a fact of life:

The American National Standards Institute (ANSI) standard "Safe Practices for Motor Vehicle Operations", ANSI/ASSE Z15.1 - 2006, defines defensive driving as "driving to save lives, time, and money, in spite of the conditions around you and the actions of others."[26]

In the same spirit, it would be nice if we exercised more care, tolerance, and vigilance in our communications and interpretation of what we hear. The goal is similar to defensive driving: to save time and money, and to reduce the frequency and intensity of disagreements, in spite of the conditions around you and the actions of others.

Another saying worth remembering in disagreements is this: "The customer is always right." This saying is usually used to remind us that the long-term relationship with a customer is worth more than a single transaction. Similarly, you might want to ask yourself whether it is worth it to sour relations with family members and colleagues for the sake of winning one argument.

Golfing, investing, and gambling are also activities known to cause serious frustration. People learn to accept setbacks and to focus on the overall results. Whatever you are doing, you don't want to get agitated or riled up and lose control. Keep things in stride when you notice you're piling on the negative thoughts. Catch yourself using negative stereotypes. We need to remind ourselves of the real costs of verbal arguments both in terms of money and in terms of our health and well-being. Accept the fact that people have different opinions that should be respected. Just as we need to share the road with others, we need to give people a chance to voice their opinions. As we saw in Chapter 2, people have different interests and priorities. Accept the fact that everyone makes mistakes. Nobody is perfect. Ambiguities and double-meanings and other mistakes happen in communications. Accept the fact that things don't always go your way. We can't control others any more than we can control the golf course, the stock market, or the dice. Take a break to cool off if necessary. Resist the urge to fight back or to stonewall. Stay calm and reasonable so you can deal with the situation in the most effective way possible.

As an example, let me share a story. Years ago, I was caught doing something stupid by a traffic cop. As he walked over to the side of my car, I could feel my heart pounding inside my chest. Despite that, I was able to control myself and calmly say, "Is there a problem, officer?" Here's the point. Even though your adrenaline may have already kicked in, it is still possible to choose how you react to a situation.

Upon hearing this story during a discussion, one wise guy asked, "So are you telling me that I should try to outrun the cops?"

I thought about it for a second.

"Not at all," I replied. "Practice at home first. Tell your spouse you found a great emotional management exercise. Explain how you have to remain calm even when your heart is pounding. Then confess to something horrible you've done recently!"

Exercise—Be Good Now!

What are some situations where you have to watch your behavior and hold your emotions and your tongue in check? For example, when you meet your in-laws for the first time, or if you find yourself in front of a judge.

———

Chances are, you have probably been downright sweet and charming in some of the situations in the preceding exercise. The next time, instead of having the usual arguments and fights with people and losing your temper, try to hold back. Once you're able to remain calm, then it's time to listen.

CUSTOMER SERVICE

Customer service is one aspect of business where the value of listening is obvious. It is critical to appreciate a customer's frustration. The following dialogue shows someone who doesn't listen properly:

"This thing doesn't work. I've spent hours on it!" I said in a huff.

"Let me see," the guy behind the counter mumbled slowly.

He examined the device for a bit. Then he slowly looked up at me and said, "Yeah, it's going to take me a few. I'll call you when I'm ready."

He nodded towards a row of seats by the wall and then turned around. A few minutes later, he called me back to the counter.

"Yeah, it's broken," he said.

When we're unhappy about something, we don't want others to stay in their relaxed frame of mind. We want them to appreciate our frustration. We don't want them to act as if nothing happened. We don't want to be told obvious things we already know, either. As listeners, whether we are dealing with complaints about us or are simply expected to address an issue, we need to acknowledge the frustration.

A customer's excitement in a new purchase should also be taken into consideration. A customer service representative can say, "I'm sorry you weren't able to enjoy our product right away," or, "I'm sorry you had to spend time getting this fixed." These responses are specific and acknowledge the inconvenience and unmet expectations. You want the customer service representative to be a good audience. You don't want them to read from a script. You don't want to feel you're being processed or rushed through customer service procedures.

THE BUSINESS OF LISTENING

I only wish I could find an institute that teaches people how to listen. Business people need to listen at least as much as they need to talk. Too many people fail to realize that real communication goes in both directions. *Lee Iacocca*

I was on an online forum when someone posed a question: "How do you deliver a high-energy keynote address on listening to a roomful of skeptical business people?" I suggested the following way to open the session:

"Do you believe in Excellence?"
"Yes!" the crowd roars.
"Do you believe in Passion?"

"Yes!" the crowd roars.
"Do you believe in Listening?"
The crowd mutters "Yes," hesitantly.

People don't always expect listening to follow excellence and passion. The question encourages people to think about the strategic importance of listening and its place in corporate culture. The truth is, all those wonderful things such as quality, excellence, service, and listening are related and reinforce one another. You can't say you believe in quality and service but you don't want to listen to the customer. You can't say you believe in listening but not in good service, either. You also can't say you listen to the customers but you don't listen to your employees.

You may ask yourself this question: "Would you like to have better company morale than your competitors?" What if you had better teamwork and cooperation in your company, both in small work groups and between large departments? Since listening is an important interpersonal skill, improving your staff's proficiency in it can give you a tremendous competitive advantage.

In general terms, the goal of your company is to help clients. Managers help subordinates succeed in daily tasks and professional growth and development. Sales people build relationships with clients and help them solve problems. Customer-facing staff provide service to customers. Everyone—including human resources, accounting and manufacturing—cooperates to achieve these goals. Again, hearing concerns and drawing people out is key.

Listening, then, is a natural part of your business strategy to strive for excellence, efficiency, teamwork, quality and good customer service. It should receive appropriate support and endorsement from the top and there should be adequate training for it. Its impact on factors such as manager performance, customer loyalty, and staff retention should also be measured appropriately.

REVIEW ME

In terms of everyday situations, virtually all companies already have formal and informal listening activities in place. For example, performance reviews are a formal way for management and staff to review issues. Whether people listen to one another, however, depends on whether anyone has anything useful to say. Are reviews just a predictable exercise with no surprises, or do people really take the time to offer specific praise and constructive feedback? The true test of a good review is when both manager and employee leave the meeting feeling better than before. This isn't just about chastising poor performers. Rather, it is about acknowledging weak areas and identifying resources and training to address them. This isn't just patting good performers on the back. It is about identifying further opportunities for professional growth. It isn't complaining about management either. It is about clarifying direction, and asking what you can do to make life easier for your manager.

Meet Me In The Conference Room

How about meetings? And why is it that no one listens at these things? Well, are meetings in your company just the battle ground for people to defend their territories, point fingers, avoid responsibility, or show off their assertiveness and opinions? Or are your meetings a place where information is shared, concerns actively solicited, and cooperation forged?

For example, if manufacturing makes a request at a meeting, asking the designers for more advanced notice, the head designer might counter with any of the following:

"You're not suggesting ways to do our jobs, are you?"

"I want to help, but it'll slow us down."

"We're only responding to customer requests."

"We tried it before and it didn't work."

You might say that the designers are acting like prima donnas. Or you might say that manufacturing doesn't appreciate that design work is inherently fluid. Either way, if defensive or adversarial attitudes are allowed to dominate meetings, then cooperative communication will obviously break down. No one will listen.

Ultimately, upper management has to recognize that there is a disagreement (or power struggle) between departments. It has to acknowledge the disagreement in a fair way and help the group resolve any differences. In this case it needs to decide what amount of manufacturing rework is acceptable in exchange for design flexibility. It also needs to make the decision known, or at least the criteria for making the decision known. That way people don't have to chase a moving target, or challenge each other's interpretation of the rules.

"Folks, nobody is here to tell anyone else how to do their jobs. No one is suggesting ignoring our customers or slowing work down or rehashing previous work. If there are ways to enhance communication between departments, then we must explore them. If we need better guidelines to lock down design changes, then let's discuss it and come to a consensus."

EXPECTATIONS, ACCOUNTABILITY

When you say you want to listen to your employees, customers, or constituents, people don't imagine that you are going to listen to them as a friend. People don't imagine that you are going to sit in silence while they tell you their ideas and concerns, feel better, and then walk away. Saying that you listen sets up an expectation that you are going to do something about the feedback.

This poses several difficulties. First, you cannot possibly satisfy everyone. Second, not all feedback is equal. Customers, employees, and citizens are not necessarily experts on business processes, service delivery, and governing. It might take some work to tease out useful, actionable items from the feedback. Complaints can certainly point to flaws that need to be fixed. But complaints don't automatically lead to good solutions.

In an article published in the September-October 1998 issue of *Harvard Business Review* titled "Right Away and All at Once: How We Saved Continental," former president and COO of Continental Airlines Greg Brenneman talked about listening to customers. Instead of asking for everything that the customers have thought about, he discussed a method to limit the amount of feedback:

> If you ask them what they want and will pay extra for, you will get a single sheet of paper with requests.

Brenneman goes on to talk about listening to employees. The key is taking steps to ensure accountability.

> Of course we'd be fools if all we did was talk at our employees. We listened too. We set up a toll-free hotline that operates around the clock to handle employees' suggestions. Pilots, flight attendants, mechanics, and gate agents manage the hotlines. They are required to research each suggestion and get back to the employee within 48 hours with one of three responses: we fixed it, we are not going to fix it, and here is why; or, we need to study it a little more, and we will get back to you by such and such date.

No Time To Listen

With everyone trying to do more with less, finding the time to listen is a genuine concern. What if you're a busy manager and you only have 10 minutes to listen to someone? To answer this question, let's ask a slightly different one: what if an employee only has 10 minutes to take care of a customer? Most people would say that servicing customers is a priority. Similarly, a manager needs to make herself available for important issues. To be fair, an employee should be able to convey the significance of an issue within the first few minutes of a discussion. If he doesn't, the manager can calmly ask, "Why do you think this is important?" or even, "Why do you think this is important right now?" If the employee can't describe the importance, but still seems agitated, there are still a few options. The manager can ask the employee to spend some time to think about the situation and return later. Or the manager can ask the employee to discuss the situation with someone else in the meantime. If it turns out that it is an issue that requires immediate attention, then obviously other matters will have to wait.

This brings up some other questions. What if someone is always complaining? Well, no one likes to listen to chronic complaining, even if it's two minutes a day. In that case, the individual needs to look for things that can be changed, and then come up with concrete actionable plans to change them.

Another situation can inhibit a manager's desire to listen. If the manager knows something is wrong or something bad is about to happen, he might not wish to risk being confronted about it. In this case, the underlying issue has to be dealt with first. For example, if you know your product is not competitive in the market, asking for feedback while ignoring obvious flaws would be counterproductive.

OTHER RESOURCES

There are a number of books that offer ways to improve our ability to handle potentially contentious communications problems. Readers can look into Marshall B. Rosenberg's *Nonviolent Communication: A Language of Compassion*; Robert E. Alberti and Michael L. Emmons' *Your Perfect Right: Assertiveness and Equality in Your Life and Relationships*; Suzette Haden Elgin's *The Gentle Art of Verbal Self-Defense*; and *Crucial Conversations: Tools for Talking When Stakes Are High* by Kerry Patterson, Joseph Grenny, Ron McMillan, and Al Switzler.

Marshall Rosenberg describes an overall process to help us express ourselves honestly and to receive empathically. He lists the four components of his Nonviolent Communication process as follows:

1. observations
2. feelings
3. needs
4. requests

He gives an example of a mother observing, and then expressing how she feels and what she needs:

"Felix, when I see two balls of soiled socks under the coffee table and another three next to the TV, I feel irritated because I am needing more order in the rooms that we share in common."

The mother then makes a specific request as described in his fourth step:

"Would you be willing to put your socks in your room or in the washing machine?"

Suzette Elgin, on the other hand, goes through a variety of remarks that goad a listener to fight back. These remarks include exaggerations, insinuations, and various put-downs. Elgin then offers ways to deflect or otherwise sidestep these provocations. Here's one example the book provides to show how to defend against a verbal attack:

Man: If you *really* loved me, you wouldn't waste so much money.

Woman: You know, it's interesting that so many men have this feeling that their wives don't love them.[27]

Crucial Conversations covers various tools and strategies to get all relevant information out into the open during risky, controversial, and emotional conversations. For example, the book discusses "Sucker's Choices":

... simplistic tradeoffs that keep us from thinking creatively of ways to get to dialogue, and that justify our silly games.

An example of a simplistic but self-limiting tradeoff is: "Either we can be honest and attack our spouse, or we can be kind and withhold the truth."[28] Another one of the areas that the book discusses is our tendency to act like victims, act like the other side is a villain, or to act helpless.

In addition, a number of books deal with more specific situations. For example, there is *How to Talk So Kids Will Listen & Listen So Kids Will Talk* by Adele Faber and Elaine Mazlish, and *Just Listen: Discover the Secret to Getting Through to Absolutely Anyone* by Mark Goulston, M.D.

SUMMARY

Our daily communications can be fraught with problems and with the potential to create arguments. Differing opinions, inaccuracies, mistakes, and plain old fatigue are unavoidable. It's helpful to adopt an attitude that takes this into consideration. Many activities in life require us to deal with random elements outside of our control and to stay calm in the face of frustration. We need to borrow the same discipline and equanimity we learn from these activities and apply them to our communications problems. Keep this in mind and you can reduce the frequency and intensity of arguments and disagreements.

Listening is integral to business strategies for excellence and customer service. Better listening can enhance a whole range of formal and informal business communications crucial for daily operations. Succeed in improving listening in your organization and you can improve morale, efficiency, and your bottom line.

Chapter 9 Better Listening In 8 Steps

Courage is what it takes to stand up and speak; courage is also what it takes to sit down and listen.
Winston Churchill

To succeed at becoming a better listener, you need tools, support from loved ones, and a plan. Before I delve into the 8-Step Listening Improvement Plan, let me do a quick recap and arm you with some more tools. There is a Listening Diagram in the Appendix that summarizes the ideas in this book. The techniques support your listening activities, which can be divided into different roles. The quickest way for anyone to improve as a listener is to be a better audience. It can be used every day and it is the basis for other kinds of listening. The most important skill is arguably the ability to put yourself in someone else's shoes and to entertain opinions different from your own. In terms of overall strategy, keep in mind that there are different ways to serve a speaker. In conflicts, remember to stay calm. Maintain your ability to listen, to understand, and to reason.

USE THE BOOKMARK, LUKE[**]

It is important to be in the right frame of mind while listening, so I have included a little device to help you. In the Appendix of this book, you will find a page that can be used to create a Listening Bookmark. Alternatively, you may download the graphics file from the Listening Tips > Resources section of www.8StepListen.com and print it out yourself. Hand the Bookmark to someone when you want them to listen to you. The Bookmark says, "Thank You for Listening." It expresses your appreciation in advance for the listener's efforts, and also serves as a blatant reminder of the title of my book—now that's a win-win! Use the Bookmark to indicate what listening role you'd like them to assume: an Audience, a Contributor, or a Counselor. On the other side of the Bookmark are some quick tips.

Try not to force people to adhere to your request. It's perfectly fine if you think you just wanted an audience but then decide that you want more input from the listener. It's also alright if you're not completely satisfied with the listening you get. The Bookmark is meant to be a light-hearted reminder. Often times it's enough just to say, "I need to go get the Bookmark."

The last thing you want to do is to keep score and track violations. "I've served you as an audience more than you've served me!" "I asked you to be a contributor and all you did was sit there pretending to listen!" As a speaker, the Bookmark reminds us that

---

[**]   Play on famous line from the movie *Star Wars, Episode IV: A New Hope*

we're the ones with a need. Remember, the key sentiment here is gratitude for the listener's efforts.

As a listener, when you see the Bookmark, it should first of all remind you of the importance of serving the speaker's needs. He or she is not asking to be advised, corrected, lectured, admonished, etc. If you have teenagers, they might even insist on using the Bookmark in all future conversations with you! Second, the speaker has indicated a preference for what he or she would like you to do. Take that into consideration as you proceed to listen. Third, if you feel it is appropriate to switch to a different role, then by all means check with the speaker.

You may continue to use the Bookmark until you become more aware of the different needs of a speaker and the different strategies to meet them. Use them as long as they promote more mindful conversations and better listening habits.

8-STEP LISTENING IMPROVEMENT PLAN

Now it's time for the 8-Step Listening Improvement Plan. The first part of the plan is to make sure you get rewarded. Let's face it, if you're anywhere as selfish as I am, then you're going to need this to stay motivated. The Appendix contains a table called "Listening Rewards". For the next few weeks, you're going to make an effort to listen to people. Each time after you listen to someone, ask them to put their initials in the column next to all the descriptions that fit.

These descriptions will help you stay focused on making it worthwhile for people to talk to you. The most important thing is not whether you paraphrased properly or used the right body language. If you heard someone else's concerns accurately, then you must have done something right. If someone felt better after speaking to you, then you were a good listener.

Try to be creative with this list of descriptions and make it work for you. For example, if you mess up and call someone's childhood passion, "a stupid waste of time", then let the speaker put an "X" or draw a sad face on your Rewards sheet. Apologize and work hard to earn the right for the speaker to explain to you why their dream is so important to them. The goal here is not to be a perfect listener, whatever that may be. The goal is to improve.

At the end of 15 weeks, you will have a collection of initials spread across the page. This is proof of the gratitude and appreciation you've earned for your time and attention. This isn't a competition to get the most initials. No matter what happens, you have already won. Your job is to keep winning the gratitude and respect of others long after the 15 weeks have ended.

Now let's talk about what you're going to do each week. Spend the first week writing down what you've learned about listening. Talk to someone you love or someone at work about your newfound appreciation of the sophistication and power of listening. Show them the Listening Bookmark and tell them they can ask you to listen to them whenever they want. Show them the Listening Diagram if necessary. Review your answers to the exercises in this book.

The next two weeks, interview three different people each week for 5 minutes apiece. It could be someone at home, someone at work, and some random person. Ask them to start with neutral topics first. For example, they can talk about something interesting happening in their lives. If they say nothing of interest is happening, then ask them to talk about a hobby, or ask them to talk about something that they would like to do that they're not currently doing. Then listen as an audience. Go to the topic "Practice asking good questions" under the Forum menu on my website www.8StepListen.com and participate.

Follow up each subsequent week by going back to the same person and use your own words to tell them what you heard last time.

Continue to listen to others as an audience for the next two weeks. Now, you may talk to each other about current affairs, issues at home, or other more serious matters. Go to the topic "Understanding Others" under the Forum menu on my website www.8StepListen.com and participate.

Next, to practice contributing to a conversation, spend one week reviewing missed opportunities in your past. Think about something good someone did at work or at home. Did they accomplish a personal goal, learn a new skill, etc.? What specific praise could you have given them? What constructive feedback could you have given them?

Next, spend three weeks giving specific praise and constructive feedback. Remember not to be over-bearing. If you don't feel comfortable expressing these thoughts or you're not sure it will come out right, then write them down first. Think of a situation where you usually tell people what to do. Refrain from giving advice; assist the other person in finding an answer instead. Go to the topic "Contributor" under the

Forum menu on my website www.8StepListen.com and participate. Each following week, go back to the same person and ask them how things went.

Remember that a counselor challenges and guides you in a compassionate way to accept, learn from, and overcome a problem. A counselor comforts, supports and encourages you to grow from the experience. To practice this, first think about how you beat the odds and achieved a goal in the past. Perhaps you never thought you'd ever repay your student loans but somehow tightened your belt and got through it. Perhaps you bounced back from an illness. How would you have reassured and encouraged your younger self to succeed? Write down your words of wisdom.

The real world provides many news events that offer an opportunity to comfort, encourage and inspire. Look at the news scandal of the week. Write one fictitious letter a week for two weeks to the person at the center of the scandal or to the victim of the scandal (or both). Acknowledge how cornered, embarrassed, guilty, or betrayed they might feel. Try to remind them of their strengths. Help them accept where and how things may have started to go wrong. Think about the constraints they're under and the possibly unpleasant choices they have to make to resolve the situation. Help them do what is right. You may post your letters and vote on other users' letters in the topic "Counselor" under the Forum menu on my website www.8StepListen.com.

Finally, spend two weeks offering support and encouragement to someone. If the opportunity doesn't come up, don't sweat it. Instead, give yourself a pep talk.

At the end of 15 weeks, reflect upon your journey. I remember with pride the times I listened and offered something useful in return. I was able to tell a colleague that more color would make his website more appealing. I was able to get a friend to think about how the relationship could serve both her and her boyfriend's needs. I was able to encourage a friend who had just started her own business and was worried about her company's cash flow. What positive exchanges will you remember as a result of these exercises?

Here's the sample schedule that I just described:

Step 1: Week 1
Write down what you've learned about listening. Review exercises in this book.

Step 2: Weeks 2 - 3
Interview 3 people each week. 5 minutes each. Start with neutral topics. Practice asking questions on website.

Step 3: Weeks 4 - 5
Interview 3 people each week. 5 minutes each. Move on to more substantial topics. Participate in "Understanding others" topic on website.

Step 4: Week 6
Review previous missed opportunities to offer specific praise and constructive feedback. Write down what you might have said.

Step 5: Weeks 7 – 9
Offer specific praise and constructive feedback.. Participate in "Contributor" topic on website.

Step 6: Week 10
Review how you overcame obstacles in the past. Write down how you would have provided support, encouragement, and inspiration to yourself.
Step 7: Weeks 11 – 13
Look at the news scandal of the week. Write a fictitious letter to one of the people involved in the scandal. Participate in "Counselor" topic on website.
Step 8: Weeks 14 – 15
Offer support and encouragement to someone. Reflect on your experiences going through the Listening Improvement Plan.

Remember after you listen to someone to return to them a week later. Confirm what you heard was correct and ask for feedback. Pay attention, ask good questions, confirm you understand, show empathy. Let people tell their story. Help them tell their story.

CONCLUSION

By entertaining my ideas, even if only for a moment, you have been my audience, and I thank you for that. The debt I owe to my parents, teachers and friends for listening to me is one I can never repay. As for my own listening efforts, they have given me a tremendous sense of pride and achievement. The feeling that your humble, selfless efforts may have made a difference to another person is something I wish everyone could experience. When you offer a bit of your humanity to someone else, much more is received in return. We live in a world where we seem all too ready at times to close our ears. And yet all of us recognize in our hearts that life would be better if we could develop more empathy and interest in other people's well-being. The world would be a better place if we were more aware of communication problems, and if we sought to minimize confrontations wherever possible.

There is no mechanical technique or simple recipe to listening. There is only caring and assisting through sincere listening. You cannot enjoy the benefits of working and being with others without taking on your share of upkeep of the relationship. In business, it means listening to other people's ideas and concerns. In families, it means you have to support one another through the frustrations and anxieties of life, the universe, and yes, one another. As the saying goes: "Nobody says on their deathbed that they wished they had spent more time at the office." However, I wish to offer something else: Nobody says on their deathbed that they should have spent more time listening to their bosses.

I can tell you listening saves marriages. I can tell you listening helps estranged fathers reconnect with grown children. I can tell you listening helps turn around businesses and brings adversarial parties back to the negotiation table. These are all valid and powerful reasons for listening. More importantly, you can have improved interpersonal relationships in the first place by using what you've learned in this book. Spend more time listening to your customers' and your children's stories. Listen to your subordinates and contribute to their daily success and to their personal and professional growth. Listen and provide support and encouragement to your loved ones. Use what you've heard to surprise people on special occasions: graduations, birthdays, Christmas, anniversaries, etc.

Use what you hear to be more thoughtful and considerate. Make it so that people *want* to share their successes, problems, and plain old questions and musings with you. Use your listening skills to make it rewarding for them to do so.

In addition, I want you to think about L. Frank Baum's *The Wonderful Wizard of Oz*. The Scarecrow, the Tin Woodman, the Cowardly Lion and Dorothy all found that they had the potential to fulfill their dreams all along. You need only to look inside yourself. I know you will find that you always had the courage, wisdom, heart, and means to be a better listener.

The more you give others by being a good listener, the more you will grow as a person. Serve the speaker's intellectual, spiritual, and emotional needs, and you will be rewarded with wisdom, compassion and joy. To borrow from President John F. Kennedy, ask not to have your frustrations and desires addressed; ask how you can better understand someone else's frustrations and desires. Ask not to be heard, ask how you can listen.

Appendix

LISTENING DIAGRAM

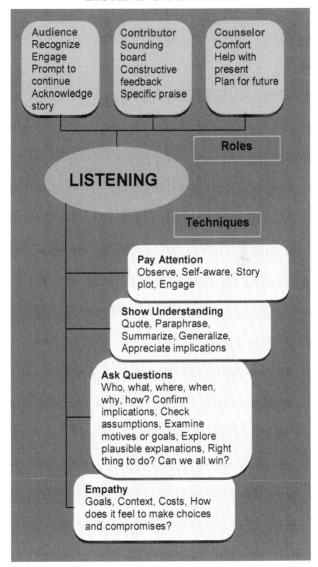

Serve the speaker's need to be entertained, informed, inspired, or touched by his or her own story.

Audience: let the speaker tell and enjoy his story.
Contributor: be a good Audience and add to the conversation.
Counselor: be a good Contributor and be supportive and encouraging.

LISTENING REWARDS

I really enjoyed our chat.	
You asked good questions. You didn't make me feel stupid.	
You made me think. You got me thinking.	
You didn't judge. You didn't make me feel bad.	
You understood what I was saying.	
You allowed me to talk through my different ideas and choices.	
Your feedback was very helpful.	
You heard my concerns.	
I really appreciate your support and encouragement.	

References

1   *Classics of Strategy and Counsel The Collected translations of Thomas Cleary*, Vol 1, Shambhala, 2001, Thomas Cleary.

2   *How to Win Friends and Influence People*, Simon & Schuster, 2009, Dale Carnegie.

3   *Seven Habits of Highly Effective People*, Fireside, 1989, Stephen Covey.

4   http://www.nytimes.com/2011/03/13/business/13hire.html

5   http://www.latimes.com/health/sc-health-0706-bad-doctor-20110707,0,4356302.story

6   http://www.nytimes.com/2011/07/11/health/policy/11docs.html

7   http://www.marketwatch.com/story/dell-commissioned-study-reveals-companies-that-listen-realize-business-results-2011-07-13?reflink=MW_news_stmp

8   http://www.dellsociallistening.com/

9   *A way of being*. Boston: Houghton Mifflin, 1980, Carl R. Rogers.

10 "Je pense donc je suis" - Discourse on Method, 1637, Rene Descartes.

11 "Therapists' Perspectives of Couple Problems and Treatment Issues in Couple Therapy", *Journal of Family Psychology*, 1997, Vol. 11, No. 3, pp361-366.

12 *Theory and Practice of Counseling and Psychotherapy*, 8th Edition, Thomson Brooks/Cole, 2008, Gerald Corey.

13 *Interpersonal Communication Everyday Encounters*, 6th edition, Wadsworth Publishing, 2010, 2007. Julia T. Wood.

14 http://en.wikipedia.org/wiki/Tell_(poker) retrieved 4/13/11

15 *Escape* (The Pina Colada song), by Rupert Holmes

16 *As You Like It*, by William Shakespeare

17 *Catcher In The Rye*, Back Bay Books, 2001, J.D. Salinger.

18 For more information on the neurological underpinnings of empathy, read *The Tell-Tale Brain: A Neuroscientist's Quest for What Makes Us Human,* Cornerstone, 2011, V. S. Ramachandran.

[19]   An article titled "Contagious yawn 'sign of empathy'" from the BBC website http://news.bbc.co.uk/2/hi/6988155.stm (retrieved on April 17, 2011) describes an experiment lead by Dr Catriona Morrison at the University of Leeds that shows that empathetic people are more prone to yawning as a result of someone else yawning.

[20]   "The Shoes of Imelda Marcos," in *The New York Times*, March31, 1986. http://www.time.com/time/magazine/article/0,9171,961002,00.html

[21]   "Don't You Think It's Time to Start Thinking," by Northrop Frye in *The Toronto Star*, January 25, 1986

[22]   "The brain's braking system (and how to use your words to tap into it)," by Dr. Matthew Lieberman, *NeuroLeadership Journal*, Issue Two 2009.

[23]   *The Last Lecture*, Hyperion, 2008, Randy Pausch, p. 67.

[24]   To read about emotional intelligence and the effects of amygdala hijacking, see *Emotional Intelligence: 10th Anniversary Edition; Why It Can Matter More Than IQ*, Bantam, 2006, Daniel Goleman.

[25]   For more information on the grieving process, see *On Death and Dying,* Scribner, 1997, Elisabeth Kubler-Ross, and *The Other Side of Sadness: What the New Science of Bereavement Tells Us about Life After Loss*, Basic Books, 2009, George A Bonanno.

[26]   American National Standard Safe Practices for Motor Vehicle Operation, American Society of Safety Engineers, Des Plaines, IL, 2006

[27]   *The Gentle Art of Verbal Self-Defense*, Barnes & Noble Inc., 1980, Suzette Haden Elgin, p.34.

[28]   *Crucial Conversations*, Kerry Patterson, Joseph Grenny, Ron McMillan, Al Switzler, 2009, Kerry Patterson, Joseph Grenny, Ron McMillan, Al Switzler, pp.38-39

Index

About The Author

Marc Wong's father was born in Mauritius. His mother was born in South Africa. He was born in Hong Kong. He has lived in Hong Kong, Canada and the United States. He first learned about listening when he volunteered at a telephone crisis center more than 20 years ago. Since then he has been passionate about the subject. He has listened to friends, listened to customers as a sales person, listened to users on a computer help desk, and listened to clients as a computer consultant. He finally decided a few years ago to give up his financially secure job configuring firewalls for the privilege of speaking and writing about listening.

For your business listening needs, connect with me at:
www.linkedin.com/in/marcwonglisten

Be a fan on Facebook:
Facebook.com/8steplisten

Follow on Twitter:
@8steplisten

Proof

Made in the USA
Charleston, SC
13 July 2012